SCHOOLS
UNDER
SIEGE

SCHOOLS UNDER SIEGE

The Impact of
Immigration Enforcement
on Educational Equity

Edited by
Patricia Gándara
Jongyeon Ee

HARVARD EDUCATION PRESS
CAMBRIDGE, MA

Paperback ISBN 978-1-68253-647-6
Library Edition ISBN 978-1-68253-648-3

Library of Congress Cataloging-in-Publication Data in on file.

Published by Harvard Education Press,
an imprint of the Harvard Education Publishing Group

Harvard Education Press
8 Story Street
Cambridge, MA 02138

Cover Design: Wilcox Design
Cover Image: Sandra Starke/EyeEm via Getty Images

The typefaces in this book are Adobe Garamond Pro and Myriad Pro.

CONTENTS

ACKNOWLEDGMENTS

T HIS BOOK WOULD NOT HAVE BEEN POSSIBLE without the contributions of many people and organizations that have dedicated themselves to creating more socially just schools and communities for the children of immigrants. We express our gratitude to the nation's educators who unwaveringly serve, teach, and advocate for children from immigrant families, and who took the time to share their knowledge and experiences with us. We have been especially inspired by those individuals working tirelessly in communities across the country to support those immigrants who make our daily lives possible. Much of the writing of this book took place around the time that COVID-19 national lockdowns began. In the midst of global chaos in which we were experiencing unprecedented changes in things we used to take for granted, there were things that never changed: essential services that we need for our daily survival. We would like to thank the workers doing these jobs, particularly immigrant workers on the front lines who risked their own lives and well-being for the benefit of us all. It is their children who are the subjects of this book and the protagonists of this nation's future. We remain hopeful that the United States will once again recall that its greatness has been built on the backs of its immigrants, both forced and free.

We also extend our appreciation to Nancy Walser, Jayne Fargnoli, and Anne Noonan at Harvard Education Press, for their extensive support as we finished the manuscript. And, foremost, we want to thank Laurie Russman, without whom this book may have never seen the light of day but for her dedication to this project. Laurie read and organized thousands of surveys and interviews, reviewed numerous drafts, and offered her astute observations throughout. Here's to you, Laurie, from the bottom of our hearts.

INTRODUCTION

PATRICIA GÁNDARA AND JONGYEON EE

N EXT TO FAMILY, school is the most important institution in the lives of children in the United States. It is where their friends are; it is a source of structure and stability in their lives; for most, it is the place outside the home where they find caring adults; and for many, especially children of immigrants, it may be the only reliable source of daily nutrition.[1] So, when family members are threatened by immigration enforcement activities such as raids, followed by detentions and deportations, children, too, are threatened and so are their schools. Some children, out of fear, don't come to school; others come but are so affected by depression, post-traumatic stress disorder, and anxiety, that they are not able to function in school.[2] Throughout recent history, but especially during both the Obama and Trump administrations, children of immigrants—even though most are American citizens—have been traumatized by the threats of immigration enforcement and also by a pervasive message that they and their families are not wanted. Under the Trump administration, the bullying of immigrant children reached a high point.[3] These children were often taunted with remarks like "build the wall," "go home," or worse.[4] Of course, most *are* already home. Born in the United States, this is the only home they have ever known.

Although a considerable amount has been written about the plight of immigrant and refugee families under the Trump administration's aggressive immigration enforcement policies, including the separation of families, caging of children, and denial of basic services, little has been written about the impact that these policies have had on the nation's schools, particularly those that serve poor children. This volume seeks to remedy that void in the literature and to bring to wide attention new research pointing to the degree to which the futures of millions of children have been put at risk, the overwhelming majority who are US citizens, but all who are guaranteed the right to an equal education by the US Constitution.

Based on original data, new analyses, and descriptive studies, the chapters in this book describe the ways that random raids and aggressive immigration enforcement have made it nearly impossible for teachers to teach and for students to learn in communities affected by these enforcement activities. Immigration enforcement has also been carried out by partnerships between local law enforcement and Immigration and Customs Enforcement (ICE) agents, a phenomenon that puts low-income communities and their schools, especially, at particular risk, given their high proportion of immigrant students. Importantly, the research also shows that students in these schools whose families are *not* targets of immigration enforcement have also been deeply affected by the disruption to their schools and classrooms and the concerns they have for their peers who are the children of immigrants. The research findings imply that the substantive impact and nature of immigration enforcement activities have been far more comprehensive than what has been reported in the media to date.

As researchers concerned with the intersection of immigration and education, we believe this is one of the most compelling and least understood problems facing the nation today. The data show that these students—our future workforce—have experienced declining academic performance and even increasing absenteeism and school dropout in the wake of aggressive immigration enforcement. The educators charged with teaching these students and attempting to close achievement gaps need help in addressing their own needs, but little emphasis has been placed on the educators' plight in the media or in school districts. They are largely left on their own to cope.

There are bright spots, however, and these include the Biden administration's renewed focus on immigration reform. On the first day of his presidency, President Biden sent to Congress a package of immigration reform proposals that include immediate amnesty for those undocumented immigrants who are farmworkers, and a pathway to citizenship for most of the 11 million undocumented immigrants in the country. In executive orders effective immediately, he called a pause to deportations for a hundred days (which was quickly enjoined by a Texas district court), a return to the Obama-era focus on "felons not families," and pledged to extend and fortify DACA. These, of course, were stopgap measures that will give way to debate in the Congress, where immigration reform has been a political football for decades. President Biden has committed to undo some of the damage wrought by Donald Trump, but a protracted struggle is likely. A burgeoning pro-immigrant movement, which includes many educators and their supporters, will have a voice in the debates. While the country waits to see what survives of the executive orders and the reform package, we include a series of policy suggestions relevant to the local, state, and federal levels to chart the course ahead into a future that makes good on the promise of an equitable education for all students, including immigrants and the children of immigrants.

ORIGINS OF THIS BOOK

Under President Obama (2008–2016), deportations rose to all-time highs.[5] This, even though one of his campaign promises was to enact comprehensive immigration reform that would include the right to remain in the United States for many who had made their lives in the country and were actively contributing to the society and the economy. At least one rationale offered for the ramped-up enforcement during the Obama administration was that if Republicans in Congress saw that the administration was serious about controlling borders, bipartisan support for immigration reform legislation would be forthcoming.[6] This, however, did not materialize. Ultimately, President Obama shifted to a more benign immigration policy of targeting undocumented individuals with criminal records rather than law-abiding parents who had lived in the country for decades ("felons not families"). In fact, the Deferred Action for Childhood Arrivals (DACA) policy and the ill-fated Deferred Action for Parents of Americans (DAPA) were both conceived during Obama's second term in response to Congress's inability to pass immigration reform legislation.

Estimates indicate that in 2017, 365,000 high school students were eligible for DACA.[7] The program allowed young people who had arrived as young children and been in the United States consistently for at least five years, who were working or in school, and who had no record of having broken the law, to remain in the country without threat of being deported—in exchange for completing a detailed set of applications and a payment initially of $465 ($495 as of October 2020). Of course, this also divulged their immigration status and family information to the federal government, something that kept many who qualified from applying. Almost a hundred thousand undocumented high school students graduate each year.[8] Many of these young people would be eligible for a renewed DACA program under the Biden administration. Since DACA status, which had been renewable every two years (each time for an additional $495), allowed students to study and work without fear of being apprehended, it is reasonable to assume that many would take advantage of a new DACA program. But this still leaves more than 6 million students, who have at least one parent or family member who is undocumented, to worry about their fate and the fate of their families.[9]

Donald Trump campaigned on undoing President Obama's policies and raised anti-immigrant sentiment to a fever pitch with his "build the wall" rhetoric. But it was the case of Rómulo Avélica-González that signaled to many that immigration enforcement had fundamentally changed. His story was published in the *Los Angeles Times* in July 2017, reprinted in local papers, carried on television nationwide; it sent shock waves across immigrant communities across the country.[10] In this case, a father who had lived in the Los Angeles area for more than twenty years, raised his US-born children there, and had just dropped his daughter off at school was followed from the school, arrested blocks away by ICE, and told he would be deported. In the latter years of the Obama administration, deportations largely focused on people with police records or those crossing illegally at the border. Now, the Trump administration was signaling that apprehensions and deportations would affect long-established residents with no criminal history or only minor infractions, even parents of US-born children, as they went about their daily business. More recently, the targeting of hundreds of undocumented persons in California in several raids was widely perceived as "payback" for the state's sanctuary policies, with one state senator quoted as saying it was "pure malice."[11] Many people have been left anxious and afraid to even to go to work. Children cry in their classrooms for fear their parents will either lose their jobs or not be home when they return from school.[12] Although the Biden administration has voiced its commitment to changing these policies, it will not happen overnight or, in the worst case, at all. Children will continue to cry in their classrooms for some time to come.

We noticed, however, that research documenting the effects of the Trump era of immigration enforcement neglected to examine the impact that these policies were having on the nation's schools. Some research has rightly noted that children who are anxious and stressed about their home situation are hardly optimal learners.[13] And many children worry about being apprehended while at school, which would certainly make it difficult to concentrate on studies. At least indirectly, reports have suggested that the children of immigrants are affected in their learning by seemingly random immigration raids. In fact, psychologists have found negative effects on cognitive development and educational progress among school-age children with unauthorized parents, even where the children are US citizens.[14] But we had no idea how extensive these effects were, or how they were being experienced by the nation's schools. Moreover, we wondered about the student who comes from a home personally untouched by these concerns but whose best friend at school is worried and anxious. Is that student worried and anxious, too? When classmates disappear overnight, does this unsettle the classroom? What about the counselors and administrators who must intervene, sometimes several times a day, with students who are acting out or decompensating in class? Or the administrator who meets with the parents seeking reassurance that the school will not turn them in to immigration agents? How do teachers, counselors, administrators, and other school personnel experience the effects of this aggressive immigration enforcement regime? Can this be thwarting efforts to improve learning and/or retain strong teachers and administrators in our most challenged schools? In addition to wanting to know how these immigration enforcement policies were affecting the schools, we also wanted to know how the schools addressed the challenges they encountered, and does this vary by region and by the political context of the states and communities?

To find the answers to these questions, we embarked on a survey during 2017–2018 to document both quantitative and qualitative responses from more than 3,600 educators in thirteen states, twenty-four school districts, and two educator networks. This book presents the findings from this survey in depth. It also draws on a number of follow-up studies and related studies to present what we believe is the first book to examine the impact of recent immigration enforcement practices on the nation's schools through the eyes of educators who have experienced it.

It is important to note that public schools in the United States that serve the children of immigrants are largely the same schools that deal with numerous other challenges. They are principally heavily segregated Title I schools that receive federal funds to address issues associated with poverty. These schools have been under enormous pressure in recent years to close the yawning achievement gaps between poor and nonpoor students, and between White and Asian students on the one hand and Black and Latino students on the other.[15] It is in this context that stepped-up immigration enforcement has been experienced by the schools that disproportionately serve immigrant students. Some would argue that the immigration enforcement regime places unreasonable, additional burdens on these schools, particularly in the absence of targeted support to address these burdens. Given the research that shows children of undocumented parents, on average, perform more poorly in school, have higher absenteeism, and graduate high school at lower rates, it can be impossible for these schools to achieve significant improvements in these students' achievement under these additional exacerbating conditions.[16] Moreover, immigration enforcement did not let up for many of these families during the coronavirus pandemic. In fact, ICE increased its activity in the hundred miles in which it is allowed to operate from the Mexican border, frightening many parents from going to their children's schools to retrieve educational materials, learning devices, and food.

Although referred to as "immigrant students," estimates indicate that at least 88 percent of the children of immigrants are, in fact, born in the United States and have US citizenship.[17] Moreover, the small percentage of students who are foreign born also have the right to a free and equal public education through high school, guaranteed by the *Plyler v. Doe* Supreme Court decision in 1982. However, none of this protects them from the negative consequences of immigration policy targeting their parents. More than 6 million children, residing in homes in which at least one family member is undocumented, live with the persistent threat of their parents' deportation as well as economic and social instability.[18] In these cases, researchers have linked the fears of deportation with poor physical and emotional health in both parents and children, even compromising family relations.[19] Several thousand children have been separated from their parents through detention and deportation, and these children appear to suffer effects similar to those of children of incarcerated parents: psychological trauma, material hardship, residential instability, and for boys, aggression. This is underscored by research specifically on US citizen children whose parents are detained or deported, who show signs of depression, anxiety, aggression, and conduct problems not evident in children who have not experienced these events.[20] Many of these children need mental health services and, of course, carry these problems into the classroom where educators must find ways to assist them.

ABOUT THIS BOOK

Following this introduction, we provide, in chapter 1, a short history of immigration enforcement in the United States as context for understanding the unprecedented reach of enforcement practices and the threat that these practices have posed in undermining efforts to provide an equitable education for all in American schools. We explain how the situation evolved and how it has affected the schools at the center of the nation's educational agenda. The historical context is important for a number of reasons: immigrant bashing has been a favorite sport in the United States since its founding, so we should not think this phenomenon is new. However, while immigrant children have been discriminated against and segregated from their native-born, English-speaking peers in the schools, there are few accounts of how the schools have been affected by enforcement practices. This is also a period of unprecedented migration—and active responses against it—all over the world. Instantaneous communication between all parts of the globe combined with more methods of transport have increased the movement of people exponentially, changing the size and nature of migration. Chapter 1 further points out that, especially for people of Mexican origin, the situation is not new. But it is more random, more broadly targeted, and affecting many more children than has been evident in the past.

Chapter 2 presents a big-picture view of the impacts of aggressive immigration enforcement that has resulted in increased absenteeism, increased behavioral and/or emotional problems among students, decreased achievement, decreased parent involvement, and a multitude of other effects on school climate and student well-being, including an increase in bullying. All of these effects, however, differ by region of the country and also by the demographics of a school. The chapter also explores these variations and how they can mitigate or aggravate the negative impacts. Chapter 3 further probes the impact of immigration enforcement, focusing on Title I schools where the federal government has been engaged for several decades in attempting to mitigate the vast inequities in American schools. In addition to describing the context of these schools and the features that make them so vulnerable, the chapter details how and why Title I schools were hit harder than non–Title I schools by threatening immigration enforcement. Title I schools with the highest percentage of English learners—children of immigrants—were the most impacted by immigration enforcement.

Chapter 4 examines the comments of almost 2,700 survey respondents who chose to weigh in, in their own words, on how this enforcement regime has affected their students and themselves. Teachers, counselors, administrators, and other school personnel describe the various impacts on students, and how their perspectives differ according to their particular jobs in the schools. It presents compelling stories of students and delivers voices of educators. We find that immigration enforcement can be experienced in various ways. One way is through its impact on individual learners and their interaction with classroom instruction. Another way is through the impact on school and classroom climate. A third way is through the estrangement of parents who come to fear contact with the schools. And a fourth way that immigration enforcement affects schools and their mission is through increased absenteeism and disenrollment.

Because absenteeism and declining enrollment is such a major issue in low-income schools especially, we have included a chapter by Thomas Dee and Mark Murphy (chapter 5), which examines the specific impact of collaboration between local law enforcement and immigration agents. The authors detail how local complicity with federal immigration officials affects Hispanic student displacement in the schools, which highly disrupts teaching and learning, and has direct impacts on school resources. Dee and Murphy also detail the demographics where this occurs most often and how these communities have responded.

The grave concerns that were expressed by educators in chapter 4 are not only about students. In chapter 6, Shena Sanchez, Rachel Freeman, and Patricia Martin explore the impacts of immigration enforcement on educators based on an in-depth qualitative study of thirty-eight educators from all corners of the United States who had responded to the 2017–2018 survey. Incorporating unpublished in-depth interview and questionnaire data, the authors pursued such questions as, Does this extra pressure cause teachers to become less effective? Does it challenge them to stay in teaching? Does it make their jobs harder? Many parts of the country are experiencing teacher shortages, which are most acute in the schools that serve immigrant and other disadvantaged students. Therefore, these questions are important to explore from an education policy perspective.

As we sought to understand the impact of aggressive immigration enforcement on the schools, we came to conceptualize this along a continuum, from activities that threaten, such as those described above, to those that support schools and students. With respect to the latter, we sought to know how educators and others have attempted to address the challenges brought about by these enforcement policies. To this end, chapter 7 recounts the ways in which school administrators from all four census regions of the country (Northeast, Midwest, West, and South) have organized to support students, and sometimes teachers, who have been caught up in enforcement. From twenty-two administrators and individuals working with community-based organizations, we heard creative and courageous stories of extraordinary commitment, support strategies, and a network operating locally and nationally, often below the radar, to help these students and their families.

We saw how schools can become a site of social justice and resistance. This chapter offers insights into what schools and districts can do, and are doing, to confront the crises in places where ICE is operating and, remarkably, in communities that exist in deeply anti-immigrant regions.

Chapter 8 offers an example of a sanctuary school that combined resources with a local university to uplift a heavily immigrant community and set its children on a path to college. Authored by Karen Hunter Quartz, Marco Murillo, Nina Rabin, and Leyda Garcia, the chapter explores how administrators in a sanctuary school have acted to shield students, teachers, and community members from the worst effects of the immigration enforcement regime. The school, in a heavily immigrant area of Los Angeles, has for several years been experimenting with a variety of policies and practices aimed at easing the fears and meeting the needs of everyone in the school community. The authors—two researchers, a lawyer, and an administrator—recount the ways that, over a decade, policies, procedures, and practices, including a legal clinic, have been created to protect their students. While the school enjoys the support of a major university with its law school and its students, it also exists in a very low-income neighborhood where dropout is common and few students typically go on to higher education. The school overwhelmingly serves students of immigrants living in poverty and in fear of ICE, yet more than 90 percent of its students go on to postsecondary education. We hope that readers will take a cue from these contributors and ask, "What might the college or university in my region be able to do to support our immigrant students?"

The coronavirus pandemic that struck the world in 2020 highlighted the vast inequities in society and, if nothing else, confirmed the ways in which we are all in this together. We hope this book exposes a problem that has affected millions of students and their futures that has been largely hidden. Regardless of the outcomes of the latest attempts to seek a solution to our broken immigration system, these children of immigrants will continue to bear the emotional scars of years of living in fear and questioning the relevance of their schooling. The injustices done to these students ripple outward to other students, to teachers, to a whole school community, and ultimately to the nation. We simply cannot afford to write off millions of students in this generation. Therefore, in chapter 9 we lay out a set of conclusions and a list of recommendations for policy makers as well as on-the-ground educators, gleaned from three years of examining data and interviewing dozens of individuals on the front lines of the immigration enforcement crisis. Perhaps that understanding, combined with the lessons learned from so many deeply committed individuals whose words resonate through these pages, can result in a more just world for these students and their schools, caught in the terrible crucible of painful, unnecessarily harsh immigration enforcement.

CHAPTER 1

Brief History of Immigration and Enforcement

Have We Been Here Before?

PATRICIA GÁNDARA AND JONGYEON EE

I MMIGRATION HAS ALWAYS been a fraught issue in the United States. While Americans have occasionally been proud to celebrate the nation's immigrant contributions, across time immigrants have also been seen as a threat to American identity; to economic well-being; and to national security. The view of immigrants as a threat to our identity has been the most persistent, while the immigrant as a threat to economic well-being was particularly salient during much of the twentieth century, and the threat immigrants pose to national security is a defining feature of immigration policy in the twenty-first century. With the devastation of the American economy as a result of the coronavirus pandemic and the loss of millions of jobs in 2020, immigrants were once again accused of filling jobs that should go to "real Americans," even though there is no evidence that American citizens want or qualify for those jobs in the fields, in the meatpacking plants, or in the specialized world of high technology.

In this chapter, we explore (1) Americans' views of immigration over time; (2) the modern history of immigration in the United States from the late nineteenth century to the present; (3) education for immigrant children, with a particular emphasis on legal battles for basic and fair access to an equitable public education, and (4) immigration and education as human rights. We also pose the following questions: Is what we have been experiencing with immigration enforcement new? Are the policies and tactics of the Trump administration an aberration in the history of the United States as an immigrant-receiving nation?

IMMIGRATION ENFORCEMENT AND IDENTITY, ECONOMIC WELL-BEING, AND NATIONAL SECURITY

Immigrants and National Identity

Even before the actual founding of the nation (1751), Benjamin Franklin, concerned with the colonial identity as Anglophiles, lamented, "Why should *Pennsylvania*, founded by the *English*, become a Colony of *Aliens*, who will shortly be so numerous as to Germanize us instead of our Anglifying them, and will never adopt our Language or Customs any more than they can acquire our Complexion?"[1]

During the period of massive immigration between the nineteenth and twentieth centuries, once again, the nation became concerned with how "inferior" immigrants from places other than western Europe would taint the national identity. Henry Goddard, a major figure in the early study of human development, was invited by authorities at Ellis Island to create a test to determine the mental fitness of aspiring immigrants arriving at the island, since immigration law at the time did not permit the entry of "idiots." The test he developed, which became a forerunner of the intelligence tests that were to become ubiquitous in the US armed forces and in schools, "examined . . . a representative spectrum of immigrants at the time [largely from southern and eastern Europe], 40% were classified as feebleminded; 60% of Jews were classified as morons."[2] Most of these immigrants were not turned away, however, as it was found, somewhat surprisingly, that with time their mental abilities tended to improve. Whether the prejudices of the times allowed Goddard to believe his findings, or if the findings, such as they were, reinforced the views of immigrants held by the average American is not known. However, it seemed to have not occurred to Goddard that the immigrants simply didn't understand English and so did not know what the test was asking of them.

More recently (2004), Harvard political science professor Samuel Huntington charged:

> The persistent inflow of Hispanic immigrants threatens to divide the United States into two peoples, two cultures, and two languages. Unlike past immigrant groups, Mexicans and other Latinos have not assimilated into mainstream U.S. culture, forming instead their own political and linguistic enclaves—from Los Angeles to Miami—and rejecting the Anglo-Protestant values that built the American dream. The United States ignores this challenge at its peril.[3]

Curiously, Huntington argues that past immigrants have, indeed, assimilated even though the constant charge against each new wave of immigration to this nation has been the fear that "they are too different from us to assimilate successfully, and so they pose an unwelcome challenge to our identity."[4] Today, as in twentieth-century America, in addition to the "they are too different" charge, the prominent refrain that immigrants take jobs away from "real Americans" is once again given as an excuse for hunting down people who have lived and worked in the United States, often for decades. But this charge is simply not true.

Immigrants and Economic Well-being

Throughout the history of the United States, the country has needed immigrants to populate its vast expanses, provide a steady workforce, and grow the economy. Today is no different. Immigrants, both documented and undocumented, hold millions of jobs, and employers contend there is no non-immigrant labor force to take their place.[5] Moreover, in many sectors of the economy, there are simply not enough immigrant workers. An article in the *Wall Street Journal* touted, "Small businesses lament there are too few Mexicans in the U.S., not too many."[6] Yet in spite of needing them, we have been once again deporting immigrants at record levels and closing our borders to new immigrants and refugees.

The native-born US birthrate has consistently dipped below replacement levels for at least the last decade.[7] It is the children of immigrants who are stabilizing the population and reviving schools that, due to lack of students, were on the brink of closure in the Midwest and the rust belt. Some population growth is critical for the health of the economy and the maintenance of benefits for the large cohort of retiring baby boomers (born between 1946 and 1964). Less than replacement levels of births augur a shrinking economy. Of course, these children of immigrants must be educated if they are to replace the workforce that is retiring (and fend off an economic slump), and it is their education that is at risk, with the harassment and deportation of their family members and the resulting impact on their schools.

Immigration and National Security

Donald Trump won the presidency in 2016 in good part by replacing the now waning fear of Middle Eastern terrorists with his promise to build a wall to hold back the "bad hombres" from Mexico who, according to him, were criminals and rapists and "bringing drugs" with the intent to harm citizens. At one point, he even charged that terrorists from the Middle East were infiltrating the border crossers, something for which no evidence could be produced.[8]

IMMIGRATION POLICY FROM THE LATE NINETEENTH CENTURY TO THE PRESENT

The federal government did not concern itself very much with immigration policy until the end of the nineteenth century.[9] Until this time, there was relatively free movement into the country, and immigration was not perceived as a major issue. However, responding to the large numbers of immigrants who began arriving in the 1880s, the US Congress passed the Immigration Act of 1882, which effectively allowed anyone to enter who was not an "idiot, lunatic, convict or likely to become a public charge."

There was, however, one racial restriction. In the same year, the Chinese Exclusion Act was passed, forbidding the entry of Chinese into the United States. Americans had such an aversion to persons of Chinese origin that Justice John Marshall Harlan, in his surprising 1896 dissent in *Plessy v. Ferguson*, allowing for the segregation of African Americans in public places, argued that the government should guarantee, "equality before the law of all citizens of the United States, without regard to race" . . . [except] "[t]here is a race so different from our own that we do not permit those belonging to it to become citizens of the United States. Persons belonging to it are, with few exceptions, absolutely excluded from our country. I allude to the Chinese race."[10]

With the exception of the Chinese, relatively open immigration continued until 1924, when general alarm over the size of the immigration flow— 20 million people between 1880 and 1920—and the fact that many were from southern and eastern Europe and viewed as racially and intellectually suspect resulted in the Immigration and Naturalization Act of 1924. The act imposed national origin quotas with very few slots allotted for non–western Europeans, with the expectation that this would limit immigration of persons outside of western Europe and especially from Asia and Africa. For this reason, many people of European extraction who claim that their ancestors came to the United States legally and therefore all others should do the same, are at least half right. Before 1924, almost every immigrant was "legal" because the concept of illegality had not yet been invented. Those who entered the country before 1924 were largely European, consisting of families attempting to start their lives over in the New World, leaving behind lives of poverty and oppression, much like immigrants today, albeit from different parts of the globe. Mexicans during the period before 1924 tended to travel back and forth to visit but not necessarily to stay, and there was little concern about what later came to be seen as a "Mexican invasion."[11]

Disposable Immigrant Labor

The Border Patrol, first established in 1924, was most heavily present along the Canadian border and focused on controlling the smuggling of liquor and Chinese nationals trying to enter the country illegally.[12] The movement of Mexicans across the southern border was not a major consideration.

However, it soon came to be, as the Great Depression began and immigrants were vilified for taking jobs away from Americans. Raids, very much like to-day, became common, and an estimated million people of Mexican descent (both Mexican and American born) were "repatriated" to Mexico during the Depression years of the 1930s.[13] Much of this was through a campaign of fear, not dissimilar from recent times.[14] Raids were announced on the radio and even from church pulpits, ostensibly to warn the immigrant com-munity, but the government expected that many people would decide to leave of their own accord rather than face deportation. One-third of the Mexican-origin population of Los Angeles left the United States during that period, urged to leave by an increasingly hostile environment and by officials who threatened them with lengthy detentions and discontinued relief aid, among other things.[15]

With the United States' entry into World War II, the country again faced labor shortages. In 1942, the Bracero program was established that brought 5 million Mexican laborers into the country over a twenty-two-year period. The program hired male workers for fixed periods of time, without their families, and without any agency regarding their working conditions, and then sent them back to Mexico when they were no longer needed. Sometimes family members came to reunite with the "braceros," but this was risky because the Immigration and Naturalization Service (INS) was deporting wives and mothers, sometimes without their children, if caught.[16] Employers who preferred to hire outside the restrictions of the program and/or had already developed networks of available labor continued to hire workers who came of their own accord, without documentation.

With the return of soldiers from the war, the need for imported workers declined, and in 1954 the INS launched Operation Wetback, which over a year's time would deport a million no-longer-needed Mexican workers back to Mexico. The program's name alone indicated Americans' perception of these workers: perhaps not fully human and easily disposable. Although de-portations continued into the 1960s, most migrants worked in the South-west—California, Arizona, and Texas—and were not a visible presence in the rest of the country. In 1964, immigrants represented the historically lowest percentage of the population in US history (about 5 percent).[17] Thus, when the Hart-Cellar Act of 1965 was signed into law as a part of the package of civil rights legislation, there was little general concern or fanfare. The act, in line with other civil rights legislation, removed the racist national origins restrictions that had been in effect since 1924 and allowed immigration from every continent. However, in a strategic move to "keep America white," conservative legislators acted to ensure that most immigration slots would go to family members of those persons already living legally in the country. Since, at the time, almost 85 percent of the US population was considered White, and less than 5 percent were Hispanic/Latino, Congress believed that the new family reunification policy would continue this demographic trend.[18] But Europeans were no longer interested in migrating to the United States in large numbers, so three-quarters of the new immigrants came from Latin America and Asia, beginning a dramatic change in the nation's demography and identity.

The 1965 act included another fateful clause. For the first time, it placed restrictions on the number of immigrants that could come in from Latin America, and it quickly reduced their number. By 1970, only twenty thousand were allowed in legally from each country including Mexico, which had been the US's primary source of imported labor (at its peak, the Bracero program alone had brought in nearly 450,000[19]). This effectively forced most migration from Mexico to become undocumented. Immigration began to accelerate again in the 1970s, and from the mid-1970s on, the United States deported nearly 1 million undocumented immigrants each year. Most of these were persons of Mexican origin.[20] At the same time, a concern was building that long-standing members of society and the US workforce, as well as US citizens of Mexican heritage, were being targeted in raids and expelled from the country without due process. In fact, "deportation" usually consisted of threatening individuals caught up in raids with detention and being banned from reentering the United States (where many now had families and homes), with the objective that they would leave "voluntarily," that is, leave by their own means without a court order, saving the INS a great deal of time, money, and effort. Only one in ten of the "deportees" was actually formally deported by the federal government between 1965 and 1985.[21]

Late Twentieth Century: Legal Rights, Documenting the Undocumented, and New Restrictions

Political progressives perceived the pervasive threats and enforcement actions as harassment of individuals lured by employers to fill jobs that had no other takers and who were provided with no protection from sudden removal. Some immigrants complained that raids would occur just before they were due to be paid, saving the employers from paying their workers. Given the obvious abuses of immigrants, the 1970s became a decade of social and legal activism on behalf of these workers. The American Civil Liberties Union, the Mexican American Legal Defense and Education Fund, the League of United Latin American Citizens, and even the Catholic Church began defending the individuals caught up in the raids in and out of court, creating a backlash against the US government. This all resulted in the clarification of immigrant rights found in the US Constitution, which included such rights as no entry into a home without a warrant, no requirement to speak to an immigration officer, and access to counsel before interrogation. With access to counsel, some were even finding that they had a claim to legal status, thus increasing the reluctance of immigrants to "self-deport" or leave voluntarily.

By the mid-1980s, things were building to a crisis once again. Millions of undocumented persons had entered the country to work, and there was a growing sense that many deserved to stay. After all, many employers had made it clear that they had no other ready workforce, especially in agriculture. Thus, the US Congress passed new immigration legislation in 1986 that would attempt to address the growing concerns and, once again, accelerate the shift in the demography of the nation. Congress passed the Immigration Reform and Control Act of 1986 (IRCA), which had three objectives:

- Sanction employers who knowingly hired undocumented workers.
- Increase border enforcement to prevent entry of new undocumented migrants.
- Provide legal status for persons who had lived in the United States for five years or more, which included 2.7 million persons, to "wipe the slate clean" of undocumented immigrants.[22]

Unfortunately, none of those objectives was accomplished because employers resisted and the INS failed to enforce employer sanctions; increased enforcement at the border was initially undermanned and underfunded; and there were already many undocumented workers who had been in the country for fewer than five years and formed a core of a new group that would continue to grow. In fact, the increasing border enforcement resulted in what scholars referred to as "border enforcement backlash" that "transform[ed] undocumented Mexican migration from a circular flow of male workers going to three states into an 11 million person population of settled families living in fifty states."[23] As crossing the border became increasingly risky and expensive, what was once a population that moved back and forth instead brought family members over and stayed. Especially after the 1970s, the Mexican-origin population was composed increasingly of family units with children, with mixed status: some US born, some legal residents, others undocumented. As undocumented migrants became more numerous and visible across the United States, attracted to new areas where jobs were plentiful and workers were needed, there was growing concern that immigration was out of control. As has been the case throughout US history, employers needed workers in hard-to-recruit industries, such as agriculture and meat processing, now in the South and the heartland, so they encouraged immigration to fill the jobs, usually at subsistence wages. In the meantime, people living in these new destinations were confronted with neighbors who did not look or speak like them, and the immigrants became scapegoats for whatever problems existed in the society. To further curb immigration, in 1991, the Congress passed new restrictions on access to federal benefits even for legal immigrants and increased the penalties for those entering the country illegally.

The Twenty-First Century and the Threat to National Security

The country was already in an anti-immigrant mode when the attacks of September 11, 2001, occurred, destroying New York's iconic Twin Towers of the World Trade Center and crashing into the Pentagon. Several of the attackers held US visas. This set in motion a virtual hysteria about immigrants, not just as takers of jobs and failures at assimilation—the familiar concerns—but as existential threats to the average American. It also revealed that the worst threats, as well as the largest portion of immigrants in the country illegally, were individuals who had overstayed visas or received a visa despite a background that suggested they should not be eligible for one. The great irony is that while the US government had been devoting billions of dollars to border enforcement to keep out Mexicans, visa overstayers outnumbered border crossers by two to one; moreover, since 2007, Mexican immigration effectively went to zero, replaced by Central Americans fleeing another wave of violence and poverty in their countries.[24]

Immediately following 9/11, the US government reorganized its entire national security apparatus and placed twenty-two different federal agencies under the newly formed Department of Homeland Security with a very large budget and greatly expanded duties. As of 2020, Homeland Security employed 240,000 individuals. Also beginning in 2001, Democrats in the Congress again began trying to pass comprehensive immigration reform, acknowledging that US immigration policy had resulted in millions of law-abiding, hardworking, mixed-status families, with parents integrated into their communities and children either born in the United States or having lived in the United States most of their lives, in a legal limbo. The escalation of immigration enforcement after 9/11 existed alongside increasing frustration with the inability to pass legislation that would have clarified the situation for these immigrants, most of whom had by that time lived in the United States for more than a decade.[25]

When President Obama came into office in 2008, he inherited this ramped-up immigration enforcement system, owing to the response to 9/11, that was actively pursuing everyone without documentation in the country, but in reality focused on Latinos. As this was already in motion, the early years of the Obama administration recorded all-time-high deportations (in part because the many employees of Homeland Security were once again doing official deportations as opposed to primarily "voluntary removals"). Some have argued that this was a strategy to bring Republicans to the table to pass comprehensive immigration reform, but if so, it backfired because President Obama was never able accomplish this.[26] In the last two years of his administration, he directed Immigration and Customs Enforcement (ICE) to only go after immigrants with criminal records in the interior and shifted the focus to border apprehensions. Children were caught up in these apprehensions, but they weren't normally separated from their parents.

So, is what we have been experiencing with immigration enforcement new? The answer is no, we have been here before. Immigrants, both documented and undocumented, but mostly Mexican or Central American, have been the targets of terrorizing raids, abuse, detentions, and removals for most of the twentieth century and almost all of the twenty-first century so far.

LEGAL BATTLES FOR BASIC AND FAIR ACCESS TO AN EQUITABLE PUBLIC EDUCATION FOR IMMIGRANT CHILDREN

A Brief History of Education for Immigrant Students

Because the United States has never had a coherent policy of immigrant integration, the public schools have mostly played this role to the extent that there has been such activity. During the nineteenth century, bilingual education programs flourished in the public elementary schools, largely in the Midwest and mostly for children of German immigrants.[27] However, the evidence suggests that the programs mostly taught the German language while teaching other subject matter in English, and the pedagogical reason for teaching German was to facilitate learning to read, ultimately in English. What is important to note is that German immigrants exerted considerable political influence over education policy to establish these programs. Initially it seemed that the right of immigrants to teach their language and culture in the public schools in their communities was not debated. However, even before the United States went to war with Germany in 1917, there had been increasing challenges to teaching any language other than English in the public schools. German speakers had been reasonably effective in fighting off these challenges, but World War I was the death knell for the German programs. The country was swept up in patriotic fervor, and it was argued that teaching children the home language was a national security problem. Presumably, a student thinking in the native language of the home would have his or her thoughts shaped to conform with the political perspectives of that language's country.[28]

At the beginning of the twentieth century, the Japanese community in San Francisco rebelled against the school district's plan to segregate the

Japanese children into an "Oriental school," which created an international incident with the government of Japan. In this case, the Japanese community was not requesting native language instruction, but rather wanted assurance that its children would receive the same quality of education as non-Asian students. After President Roosevelt's intervention, the school district backed down and allowed the Japanese children to attend their local schools.[29]

Many states passed legislation prohibiting the teaching of, or in, other languages, but the case of *Meyer v. Nebraska* made it all the way to the Supreme Court in 1923. The court found in the due process clause of the Fourteenth Amendment the right for parents to choose to have their children taught another language in addition to English. This settled the question for the moment, but the issue of language of instruction would continue to be divisive and tied to attitudes about immigration until the present day (note the Huntington statement from 2004 in this chapter).

After the turn of the twentieth century, a general concern was growing that the huge number of new immigrants who did not speak English, and whose customs were different from the now-assimilated western Europeans of the previous century, needed to be integrated into American society if they were to be productive and patriotic citizens. Civil society and the public schools mainly undertook the task.[30] Some schools in immigrant-receiving areas of the country offered "Americanization" programs in which all immigrant students were required to enroll. While these programs could be coercive, drilling students in correct pronunciation of English words to the point of manually twisting the students' jaws, and admonishing them to leave behind all cultural practices associated with their family's country of birth, their intent, ostensibly, was to ease the students into their new culture, and thus they at least tacitly acknowledged that they were now "new Americans."[31] Those programs were largely abandoned after 1920 with the dramatic decline in immigration and substantial pushback from aggrieved immigrants. For most "immigrant" students (those who arrive at school not speaking English) today, the only means of integration into the new society is some form of English acquisition program that assumes students will leave behind their native language. The issue of bilingual instruction as a means of facilitating the education of English language learners (AKA immigrant students) has never been adequately resolved and remains a contentious issue. It also plays a central role in the support of students and families caught up in immigration enforcement, as discussed in chapter 7. It is difficult to engender trust when people cannot communicate in the same language.

Given that US immigration policy with respect to Mexico had largely focused on importing and then deporting low-wage workers, generally young males, little attention was given to the plight of their children over time. However, as more immigrant families began to settle on the US side of the border in the latter years of the twentieth century, increasing numbers of children were showing up at school speaking a language other than English (usually Spanish), and needing to be integrated into a school system that was foreign to them.[32] An estimated 6 percent of US students in 1970 were children of immigrants (most speaking another language at home), and by 2018, 26 percent were. Currently, nearly 90 percent of children of immigrants are born in the United States, but 16 percent of all first graders today come to school not speaking English.[33]

Almost fifty years after *Meyer v. Nebraska*, the Supreme Court ruled again in 1974 on behalf of children of immigrants who did not speak English in a landmark case, *Lau v. Nichols*. In this case, 1,856 Chinese-speaking students sued the San Francisco schools for failing to provide them with equal access to education because no accommodations were made for the fact that they could not understand instruction taught only in English. The high court found that the school district had violated Title VI of the Civil Rights Act by discriminating on the basis of national origin and that these immigrant students had a right to the same education as all other students. The *Lau* decision was not specific about the appropriate remedy, but many educators concluded the remedy that made the most sense was bilingual education.

Today, these English language learners are normally integrated into school via a language assistance program of some sort—it might be a teacher's aide who comes into the classroom to assist with translations for a few hours a week, a full-on bilingual program, or something in between, depending on the language resources of the school. Students who arrive in high school may encounter no additional support in the worst case, or in the best case may be assigned to a school like the Internationals Schools that are dedicated specifically to immigrant students and getting them successfully to high school graduation.[34] Some school districts offer "newcomer programs" that orient newly arrived students to US schooling expectations and routines, and usually provide initial classes in English language before mainstreaming them into regular classes. For the most part, however, the United States does a very poor job of immigrant integration, even for children. Recent scholarship has documented the social and psychological impact of migration on children and uncovered deep-seated problems associated with the parents' loss of home, the travails of the migration process and often family separations, as well as adaptation to a new country.[35] This scholarship has also pointed to the extraordinary resilience of many of these immigrant students, including elevated levels of achievement motivation.[36] In spite of our knowledge of these issues, however, policy makers and practitioners have paid relatively little attention to these children's social and psychological needs and assets. The focus of education for immigrant students is primarily on English language acquisition.

The Fourteenth Amendment, ratified in 1868, gave automatic citizenship to any person born or naturalized in the United States. Thus, regardless of the parents' citizenship status, all children born in the United States are due all the rights and privileges of citizenship, which includes a free public education. Battles have raged over how to educate those pockets of non-English-speaking children of immigrants, whether bilingually or with "a cold bath of English," and whether to segregate them from "American" children, but there was little talk of "sending them back" until immigration began to pick up again in the 1970s. Immigrant children became a more noticeable presence in the schools, especially in Texas, which passed a law denying access to public schools for noncitizen children of immigrants. This resulted in the Supreme Court's 1982 decision in *Plyler v. Doe*, which found that all children under eighteen years of age were entitled to a free public K–12 education, regardless of citizenship status. The court's reasoning was that "these children can neither affect their parents' conduct nor their own undocumented status . . . The deprivation . . . of education takes an inestimable toll on the social, economic, intellectual, and psychological wellbeing of the individual, and poses an obstacle to individual achievement."[37] In fact, the decision went on to note that denying these students access to education benefited no one—neither the state nor the individual children. The right has been tested several times in various states, but the courts have always upheld it. The *Plyler* decision is particularly relevant to the circumstances that immigrant students face today, where their access to an equitable education is severely challenged by immigration enforcement activities.

Changes After 9/11: Escalating Immigration Enforcement

The concept of families and law-abiding individuals as targets of immigration control and enforcement is relatively new in recent times, starting during the post-9/11 period under the George W. Bush administration and peaking in the first years of the Obama administration. As President Obama was pilloried by progressives and especially Latinos for the increasing deportations, he shifted to a "felons not families" policy and, in 2012, introduced the Deferred Action for Childhood Arrivals (DACA) program to allow individuals brought to the United States at a young age to remain in the country and work or go to school. The authorization was renewable every two years, but President Donald Trump attempted to end the program in September 2017, effective in March 2018, leaving hundreds of thousands of young immigrants in limbo once again. Several lawsuits challenged this attempt, and it ended up in the Supreme Court. In June 2020, the court struck down President Trump's attempt to end the program on the basis of his failure to provide a rationale for doing so. Although he vowed to go back to court and successfully end the program, he did not do so, but neither had Homeland Security accepted any new applications as the court had instructed. President Biden has reinstated the program, but the contours of its future are not yet known. At its inception, about 160,000 high school students were DACA recipients. Today it is estimated there are more than 1.3 million people who would be newly eligible for DACA with the continuation of the program.[38] The Biden administration has asked Homeland Security to "preserve and fortify" DACA, but what this actually will mean is not clear. The program could be updated and broadened to cover more individuals who just missed the cut-off dates set in 2012. And this would make sense, given the reasoning in *Plyler* that "these children can neither affect their parents' conduct nor their own undocumented status" and that it benefits neither them nor the society to deny them the opportunity to study and contribute to the American economy. The only reason to do so is for political gain, but even at that, polls show Americans support the DACA recipients by a very wide margin.[39]

Immigration Enforcement in the Trump Era

From the time that Donald Trump launched his campaign for the presidency with anti-Mexican rhetoric and the call for a wall on the southern border, all immigrants have come under attack. Day by day, the screws tightened on both documented and undocumented immigrants and would-be refugees, culminating in historic numbers of families affected and the resulting impact on the nation's most vulnerable schools. The election of Donald Trump created greater urgency to resolve the immigration issues, as his rhetoric combined with his actions became virulently racist. He famously called Mexican immigrants rapists and criminals, and labeled people from Muslim nations as terrorists to incite fear in American citizens and to gain their support for his harsh tactics. He redirected ICE to track down law-abiding immigrants in the interior and threatened "sensitive" areas like schools and places of worship. He pardoned Maricopa County sheriff Joe Arpaio for disobeying a federal court order to stop racial profiling Latinos. Arpaio had long stood as a dangerous symbol of harassment and abuse of the Latino community, and President Trump's pardoning of him was a direct affront to Latinos, both immigrants and citizens. In 2018, the Trump administration announced a "zero tolerance" policy (for unauthorized border crossing) that included separating children from their parents, which it did to thousands of children who were sent all over the country to detention centers or caregivers.[40] The single largest immigration raid in one state occurred on the first day of school in Mississippi, four days after the August 2019 anti-immigrant attack at an El Paso Walmart left almost two dozen Latino shoppers dead. The assailant, a young White male, had written a screed against immigrants before the attack; in it, he paraphrased some of Trump's rhetoric.

The Trump administration resurrected in 2019 the "public charge" threat to deny a green card (legal permanent residency) if applicants used or *could possibly* use in the future (in the judgment of ICE) any federal government benefits. Given that undocumented immigrants are ineligible for almost any federal benefits, this would not likely affect many people immediately, but it had a chilling effect on millions of people unsure of the policy's reach.[41] We heard from many school administrators that parents feared using any services that their children were legally entitled to under penalty of losing the opportunity to get a green card.

To summarize, although the children of immigrants have been buffeted by immigration policies affecting their parents, there has been relatively little attention directed at their well-being, other than to give them a right to school and some kind of language assistance. There has been almost no acknowledgment of the ways in which existing immigration policies put their right to schooling at risk, even though the great majority of these students are US citizens. As we show in chapter 4, many of these students are too stressed to pay attention in school, many fear leaving home to go to school, and many decide to leave school altogether or forgo college because their families are desperate and their futures uncertain. While immigrant children's lives have long been tenuous, owing to immigration policies that do not consider their welfare, the Trump administration raised the fear and bullying of these children to unprecedented levels.

With the transfer of the presidency to Joseph Biden in January 2021, immigration enforcement opened a new chapter. He promised relief from targeting law-abiding immigrants and a temporary pause on deportations. It is yet unknown what specific new policies will eventually be implemented; it is worth noting that the Congress has grappled unsuccessfully with immigration policy for decades. But one thing is certain. The heightened stress and fear that the children of immigrants and their schools have endured over the years of Donald Trump's presidency will not be quickly erased. Negative anti-immigrant sentiments—and actions—have been set in motion, and it will take time to reverse the momentum, heal the wounds, and allow these students to feel safe from bullying at school. It will take time to restore confidence in students that their parents will still be there when they return home in the afternoon. It will also take time to restore confidence in their future so that they are ready once again to plan to go to college and pursue their dreams. As mental health professionals tell us, it will also require therapeutic interventions for many students—and some educators—to recover from the impact of a pandemic that has isolated them in circumstances of economic privation as well as the threat of immigration enforcement. There is a long road ahead. And in a worst-case scenario, thousands if not millions of Trump supporters are waiting for the opportunity to reinstate his immigration policies in a future administration.

IMMIGRATION POLICY AND HUMAN RIGHTS

The history of immigration policy in the United States has followed a bumpy but predictable road. During periods of economic stability and relatively low immigration, laws are relaxed or rarely enforced, and immigrants, if not always welcomed, are at least tolerated. However, in less economically stable times, when immigration rises to a generally noticeable level, or in the event of some external threat (e.g., coronavirus, 9/11), Americans feel threatened and there is pressure to escalate enforcement, shut the borders, and frighten immigrants into leaving. During the month of March 2020, as the coronavirus was raging through the country and many undocumented workers were told to stay on the job as "essential workers" in meatpacking plants and agriculture where they became infected, ICE deported almost eighteen thousand people.[42] While the whole world worried about the pandemic, the continuing impact of immigration enforcement receded to the background in the minds of most Americans. But, even as the children of immigrants struggle to salvage what they can of their truncated educations, they have continued to worry if their parents will come home at the end of the day and if they will have a future in this, their country.

Immigration has indisputably been good for the United States; assessed over the long run, immigrants give back more than they take.[43] From a human rights standpoint, the children of immigrants must be educated equitably, as provided in the US Constitution, and their schools should be protected from the impact of aggressive immigration enforcement for the students' well-being and the well-being of all Americans. It is now the challenge of educators and policy makers to ensure that this happens.

CHAPTER 2

Surveying the Nation's Schools

The Impact of Immigration Enforcement

JONGYEON EE AND PATRICIA GÁNDARA

T HE UNITED STATES, under the Trump administration, became a very hostile place for immigrants, and given that 25.9 percent of all students are the children of immigrants, this constitutes a significant challenge for schools across the nation.[1] Schools are complex ecosystems that are affected by social changes and reflect the impacts of the changes on school members, including students, their parents, and educators. Given the substantial portion of students from immigrant homes in American schools and inevitable repercussions of immigration enforcement on those students and their communities, it is imperative to investigate how schools have been affected by stepped-up immigration policies of the Trump government. In this chapter, we introduce the national survey we conducted in 2017–2018 to examine the impact on the nation's schools and report the overall findings. More than 3,600 educators from 13 states and over 760 schools took part in the survey, which asked educators to evaluate the extent to which they observed adverse reactions to enforcement activity among students and parents that could affect both teaching and learning in their schools.[2] The survey also asked whether educators attempted to address the immigration issues with parents or community members.

The survey was administered between late October 2017 and mid-January 2018 and between August 2018 and September 2018 through an online survey tool. Since then, the COVID-19 pandemic has added multilayered risk factors to the stress and trauma of immigration enforcement, directly jeopardizing even further the well-being of those communities and their schools.[3] Many of the families from the schools we surveyed work in low-wage, high-risk occupations where they are considered essential workers and, as such, are at higher risk of contracting the virus than workers in other fields. While we did not survey educators during the pandemic, we talked with many in spring 2020 who offered their thoughts about the impact of the pandemic on this already vulnerable population. (We share more about this in interviews discussed in chapter 7.) This chapter seeks to answer the following questions:

1. How have educators across the nation perceived the effects of immigration enforcement on their students since President Trump took office?
2. To what extent does the impact on students and schools vary by location (e.g., region, urbanicity, and political landscape)?
3. To what degree are the effects linked to school demographic composition?
4. To what extent does the role and school grade level of the educators impact their perceptions?

DESCRIPTION OF THE SURVEY

How We Developed and Collected the Survey Data

We based the survey on careful reading of media accounts reporting the impact of immigration enforcement in communities across the country as well as on the academic literature on migration and immigrant students. The survey particularly focused on four key areas that we found both in the media articles and in academic studies: students' psychosocial stress, academic challenges, school/classroom climate, and parental involvement (see chapter 4 for further discussions on each topic). Focusing on the four themes, we specifically delved into the effects observed for central aspects of student behaviors and schooling, including students' expression of concerns and fears, behavioral and/or emotional problems, absenteeism, academic performance, indirect effects on classroom climate, indirect effects on other students (peers), bullying, parents' expression of concerns at school, and parental involvement (see the appendix at the end of this chapter).

The survey started with a question asking if the educators had observed any impact of immigration enforcement at their school or in their classroom. For those who reported that they did not observe any impact, the survey ended because the rest of the survey questions were only relevant to the scope of reportable observations by the respondents. Consequently, of the total respondents, nearly 27 percent reported that they had not observed any impact at their school, leaving approximately 3,900 (73 percent) who indicated they had or might have observed an impact. Not every respondent finished the survey, leaving responses completed by about 3,650 educators.

Next, respondents were asked to assess the degree to which they noticed an impact on each behavior using a five-point Likert scale, with one being "no impact" and five being "extensive impact." In addition to these quantified questions, an open-ended question in the survey allowed respondents to describe their observations of the impact on enforcement activities on students; and these responses are discussed in chapter 4. The survey also examined educators' attempts to reach out to the community at the individual and school levels regarding immigration enforcement issues and documented their occupational role in the school as well as the grade levels of the school where they worked, if applicable. Because we know that districts are reluctant to commit their staffs to additional uncompensated work, we constructed the survey to be concise. This also helped to ensure that school personnel would complete it. The appendix contains the survey questions used for this study.

The dissemination of the survey was carefully guided to ensure three factors. First, we wanted the data to have representation from the four US census regions, including the West, Midwest, Northeast, and South. As table 2.1 shows, the survey included educators from 13 states and over 760 schools.

Second, we developed a data collection plan with the goal of surveying one-third secondary and two-thirds elementary schools, as there are more public elementary schools in the country, and they have fewer educators. However, as we worked with multiple districts to list potential schools for survey participation based on our sampling plan, some wanted to suggest schools that they felt were more critically affected by immigration issues. Due to this bilateral selection process with some districts selecting schools, the final sample had a disproportionately high percentage of Title I schools (90.3 percent). This was not surprising since immigrants tend to be clustered in low-income communities with Title I schools. In terms of school level, we received responses from an extensive representation of schools: 38 percent of the respondents came from elementary schools, 12 percent from PreK–8 or K–12 span schools, and 50 percent from secondary schools, which included both middle and high schools (see table 2.2). With respect to various roles of educators, we grouped them into four categories: principals or administrators, teachers, other certificated educators (e.g., school psychologists, counselors), and paraprofessional or other school personnel.

Third, we wanted to include schools with varying percentages of immigrant students. However, since schools do not document immigration status of students and their parents, we adopted the share of Hispanic students

TABLE 2.1   List of states and number of schools that participated in the survey

REGION	STATE	SCHOOL COUNT
Northeast	Massachusetts, New Jersey, and New York	74
South	Florida, Georgia, Maryland, Tennessee, and Texas	240
Midwest	Indiana and Nebraska	59
West	Arizona, California, and Oregon	384
Total		**757**

Source: The immigration survey data.

Note: School counts reported in the table only include the schools identified by respondents. Therefore, the actual number of schools in the survey is estimated to be higher than 760.

TABLE 2.2   Characteristics of schools and educators in the survey

REGION	SHARE OF RESPONDENTS*
Northeast	8.5%
Midwest	22.1%
South	10.8%
West	58.7%
JOB TITLE	
Principals/administrators	8.5%
Teacher	71.8%
Oher certificated	9.5%
Paraprofessional/other staff	9.1%
District*	1.1%
GRADE LEVEL	
Elementary	38.0%
Elementary/secondary	11.8%
Secondary	50.2%
TYPE OF AREA (LOCALE)	
City	57.3%
Suburban	38.9%
Town	0.7%
Rural	3.0%

Sources: The immigration survey data; NCES Common Core of Data, 2015–2016.

* Respondents refer to individuals who completed the survey. A small number of district personnel participated in the survey, but we did not include them for our analyses. The share of respondents for each category shows percentages of the total individuals in the survey.

as a proxy for immigrant students.[4] Using a percentage of Hispanic students in the school, we ensured that the survey covered each of three groups:[5]

Group 1. The share of Hispanic students in school is < 20 percent.

Group 2. The share of Hispanic students in school is ≥ 20 percent but < 50 percent.

Group 3. The share of Hispanic students in school is ≥ 50 percent.

How We Examined the Data

The survey we created explored nine areas described in the previous section, including students' expression of concerns and fears, increased behavioral and/or emotional problems, absenteeism, academic performance, indirect effects on classroom climate and on other students, bullying, parents' expression of concerns at school, and decreased parental involvement. In addition to the survey response data, we used National Center for Education Statistics (NCES) data to understand school characteristics in interpreting survey data results.[6] Merging the survey data with NCES data, we examined aspects of schooling affected by immigration enforcement issues by region and school location, and to what extent the impact was associated with other school factors, such as student demographics, percent English language learners (ELLs), school size, grade level, educators' roles, and Title I status. We included the share of ELLs and a school's Title I status because we wanted to assess the strength of educators' responses by the percentage of probable immigrant students and by the poverty level in the school. (In the next chapter, we discuss the critical importance of Title I status and what we know generally about these schools and the challenges they face.)

We took various approaches to analyze the data. First, we grouped responses according to those who reported *any* impact (2–5 on the Likert scale) and those who reported a substantial impact (4–5 on the same scale) on each aspect of schooling to capture educators' overall observations of the impact as well as the level of impact they reported. Second, since all nine key behaviors the survey examined were organically associated with one another and contributed to a latent phenomenon that this study investigated (i.e., the overall impact of immigration enforcement), we found it important to assess a comprehensive impact of all aspects combined as well as each aspect of student and parent behavior. For exploring the comprehensive impact, in particular, we pooled responses for the nine questions together and generated a variable that reflects an average score of all nine responses. (A further explanation of this approach is discussed elsewhere.[7]) Using this average impact of all nine behaviors, we were able to evaluate the effects on schools by varying characteristics of the schools, such as role of the educators, student demographics, Title I status, school size, grade level, and school location.[8] Next, we used the merged data sets (the immigration survey and NCES data) to answer whether region of the country or urban versus suburban contexts show differences in immigration enforcement impact. Finally, we wondered if we would find differences in impact by political context—red states versus blue states, or politically conservative versus more liberal communities. For this, we analyzed four states in our data (California, Oregon, Tennessee, and Texas), located in a similar or different statewide political landscape, and then compared responses from the three states to those reported by educators in California.

HOW DO EDUCATORS PERCEIVE THE EFFECTS OF IMMIGRATION ENFORCEMENT SINCE PRESIDENT TRUMP TOOK OFFICE?

In figure 2.1, we give an overview of educators' observations for each topic we explored and presents educators' responses regarding the impact of immigration enforcement on behaviors of students and their parents. This figure also illustrates the share of respondents who identified the impact as being "a lot" or "extensive," which we considered to be a barometer of how seriously educators identified each issue.

Psychosocial Stress

Of all nine topics, the most troubling finding is that nearly 85 percent of educators noted "students expressing concerns and fears at school," with 44 percent of respondents reporting that students' fear of an ICE intervention was "a lot" or "extensive," implying that educators perceived an acute level of impact. This overwhelming share of educators reporting anxiety and stress among their students is also corroborated by countless open-ended comments from respondents that recount the fear and helplessness expressed by their students. For instance, educators reported students worrying about potential deportations of their parents, siblings, or students themselves and about their parents losing jobs that sustained the household. Respondents also observed students' declining academic motivation and feelings about their uncertain future. Furthermore, 80 percent of survey respondents noticed an increase in "students' behavioral and/or emotional problems," including students' shutting down, coming to school crying, not engaging in class, refusing to eat, and even attempting suicide. Of course, students expressing such intense

FIGURE 2.1   Impacts of immigration enforcement as reported by respondents

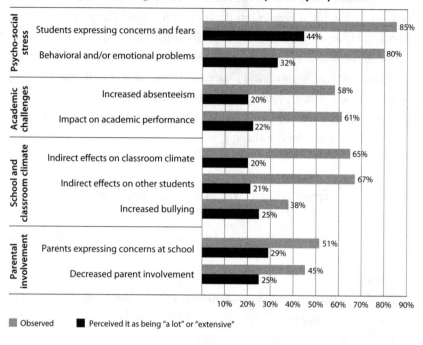

■ Observed   ■ Perceived it as being "a lot" or "extensive"

Source: The immigration survey data.

Note: The gray bar shows the shares of respondents who observed the changes for each topic; the black bar refers to the percentages of respondents who observed each impact to be "a lot" or "extensive" on the five-point Likert scale with 1 being "no" impact and 5 being "extensive."

levels of psychological and social stress, and showing emotional and behavioral problems, also affect other students in the classroom, as well as their teachers. Given that so many of the respondents considered this impact to be extensive, we conclude that these psychosocial stressors likely interfere with the ability to concentrate on class lessons, which, of course, is what hundreds of educators told us. We will revisit this topic in chapter 4 where we present in greater depth the comments shared by educators.

Academic Challenges

Nearly 60 percent of educators observed "increased absenteeism," which is often associated with a host of adverse academic outcomes, such as being unable to keep up with class instruction as well as declining test scores and ultimately dropping out of school over the long term. Growing absentee-ism also results in a critical loss of school funding calculated by students' average daily attendance. This is a particularly severe issue for Title I schools that suffer from a constant shortage of funding. (We examine this issue and others specific to Title I schools in chapter 3.) In addition to increased absenteeism, over 60 percent of respondents on average reported an "impact on academic performance" of their students. These high percentages of educators observing decreases in academic performance call attention to the widespread disruption experienced by students and schools in all regions. Like decreased attendance rates, this issue also brings a critical institutional burden on schools if overall test scores decline, which can be closely linked with the federal funding eligibility for high-poverty schools (see chapter 4) and is especially demoralizing for teachers who are held to account for their students' test scores.

School and Classroom Climate

Two in three educators in the survey reported "indirect effects on the class-room climate" and "indirect effects on students due to concerns for their peers" from immigrant families. If a student arrived at school weeping, or the student disappeared for several days due to an ICE action, other students in the same classroom would show concern and be affected. These indirect effects on the school community are the unavoidable outcome of a series of impacts that stem from soaring psychosocial stress among immigrant children. Moreover, close to 40 percent of respondents reported "increased bullying" of immigrant students, creating insecurity and anxiety, both tre-mendously detrimental to their schooling as well as their mental health, and causing students to feel as though they are unwanted and do not belong.[9] Educators' concerns about growing incidents of verbal attacks against mi-nority students—Hispanic or Muslim students—stood out.

Given that some students experience verbal and physical assaults in pub-lic spaces outside of educators' radar, such as on the way to and from school, bullying may be more widespread than what survey respondents report. We wanted to investigate this further to see how school demographics transect the overall impact of immigration enforcement specifically related to in-creases in bullying. Figure 2.2 displays the results of these analyses.

FIGURE 2.2   **Increased bullying**

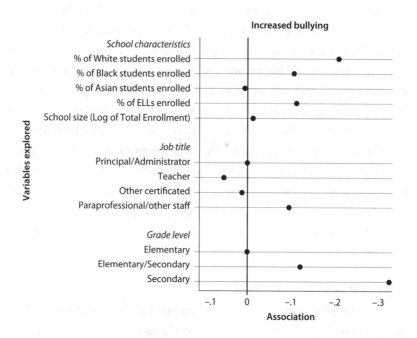

Note: Variables used for this analysis are standardized to put different variables on the same scale with a mean of 0 and a standard deviation of 1. The *x* = 0 baseline represents the standardized mean of the result.

Dots in the figure represent a magnitude (or coefficient) for each variable. Each dot's placement in the figure shows the extent to which the variable is associated with increased bullying after holding the other variables constant. For percentages of White, Black, Asian, and ELL students and school size, the more the dot is placed to the right, the greater the extent to which the variable is associated with bullying.

After adjusting for other school characteristics, such as student demographics and grade levels, increased bullying was significantly and positively associated with the share of White students in the school (see the figure). As the percentage of White students goes up in school, educators are more likely to observe increased incidents of bullying. Of course, this does not mean that White students necessarily cause this impact, only that the presence of more White students is *associated* with increased bullying.

We found that another critical factor in reporting increased bullying was educator job title and grade level (see the figure). Secondary school educators, for example, were more likely to report increased bullying than their counterparts in elementary schools. Paraprofessionals also reported increased bullying at a magnitude or extent much greater than teachers did.

As we have noted, there is considerable evidence that the Trump administration's anti-immigrant policies and rhetoric resulted in more anti-immigrant bullying in schools. What these data add to that finding is that in schools with many immigrant students, all students are affected, whether indirectly or directly, by threats against immigrant populations. Hence, enforcement activities degrade school climate in a particularly comprehensive way.

Parental Involvement

The repercussions of immigration enforcement are extended not only to students but also to parents. Almost half of respondents noted that parents had approached them with particular concerns, seeking advice or expressing fears about their family's vulnerability. A similar percentage of educators reported observing "decreased parental involvement," a vital element for schools to successfully educate children. Some immigrant parents fear interactions with the school and do not even apply for school lunch programs, which hampers the overall health and well-being of their children. This can also result in schools becoming ineligible for Title I funds, which is computed on the basis of the number of students who apply and qualify for free and reduced-price lunch.

Reaching Out to the Community

One major topic supported by an overwhelming majority of respondents in the survey—without any regional differences—was the expressed need to discuss immigration issues with the community at the school level. Nearly 90 percent of educators reported that their school needed to conduct outreach to the community regarding immigration and enforcement issues. Many educators do not feel qualified to provide accurate advice to students and parents and want to hand this responsibility on to experts. Moreover, the frustration of educators was palpable in their comments with respect

TABLE 2.3   Attempts to discuss immigration concerns

	ALL	NORTHEAST	MIDWEST	SOUTH	WEST
Need to discuss immigration issues at the school level	88.3%	90.7%	87.7%	88.4%	88.1%
Attempted to discuss immigration issues at the individual level	39.1%	45.3%	31.1%	38.5%	39.9%
Attempted to discuss immigration issues at the school level	41.8%	44.9%	45.4%	36.0%	43.0%

Source: The immigration survey data.

to the misinformation that travels through the community and results in reduced school attendance and in students losing benefits they are eligible to receive, like free and reduced-price meals. Despite such broad consensus across the regions, the absence of schoolwide discussions to support immigrant students was common. As table 2.3 shows, more than half of respondents reported that such meetings did not take place. Of respondents in the South, only 36 percent said that their schools had initiated this kind of outreach with their community, perhaps indicating the increased difficulty of doing so in a broadly anti-immigrant regional context. Yet, a slightly higher percentage (39 percent) of educators in the South had an individual-level discussion with parents. In both the Midwest and West, educators were more likely to attempt to address this topic at the school-community level.

DO THE IMPACTS OF IMMIGRATION ENFORCEMENT VARY BY LOCATION?

Although the impacts observed by educators were, by and large, extensive in schools we explored, we took a deeper look at our data to examine whether varied political or geographic contexts mattered. One of the questions we sought to answer was whether students and schools in some areas of the country were more impacted than in others. To explore this question, we probed our data with a special emphasis on (1) the four census regions, (2) different or similar political landscapes, and (3) urban and suburban contexts.

Regional Variations

Educators in all schools in our sample report observing a significant impact of immigration enforcement. Yet, we noticed some regions reported greater impacts than others. Southern and northeastern educators' responses stood out, in particular, compared to responses reported by western and midwestern educators. As table 2.4 demonstrates, of educators who reported observing students' psychosocial stress, the shares of northeastern and southern respondents who perceived this as being "extensive" were higher in comparison to the percentages for the West and Midwest. For example, over 50 percent of educators in southern schools reported observing students overtly expressing concerns and fears as "extensive," and this was nearly 20 percentage points higher compared to the responses of educators in the Midwest. Similarly, more than one-third of educators in these two regions (the South and Midwest) reported increased behavioral or emotional problems as "extensive." It is also worth noting that educators in the Midwest tended to report somewhat lesser impacts across all behaviors than other areas of the country. We speculate that this is at least partially due to sampling. The midwestern districts that chose to participate had long dealt with enforcement issues, including raids in their or nearby communities. As a result, they had developed plans and infrastructure to address these issues, which we suspect affected the overall climate of the schools. We address this issue further in chapter 7.

Academic challenges were also more prominent in the Northeast and South than in the other two regions. More than 66 percent of southern educators reported increased absenteeism, compared to 50 percent of educators from the Midwest. Similarly, while 64 percent of northeastern educators reported increases in absenteeism, 27 percent ranked this as "a lot" or "extensive." Southern educators were again more likely to report declining academic performance, with 68 percent observing this issue, compared to 60 percent of educators from the West, and 53 percent of midwestern educators. A higher percentage of northeastern educators (65 percent) also reported decreasing academic performance.

With regard to school climate, similar percentages of respondents from all regions except the Midwest observed indirect effects on classroom climate due to concerns for classmates and peers. For instance, indirect effects

TABLE 2.4   Impacts of immigration enforcement by region

	NORTHEAST		MIDWEST		SOUTH		WEST	
	Observed	Extensive*	Observed	Extensive	Observed	Extensive	Observed	Extensive
Psychosocial stress								
Students expressing concerns and fears	85.8%	48.5%	82.4%	33.2%	85.5%	52.3%	84.4%	41.3%
Increased behavioral and/or emotional problems	81.4%	36.1%	76.2%	23.2%	81.4%	35.6%	79.2%	30.7%
Academic challenges								
Increased absenteeism	64.0%	26.6%	49.9%	9.7%	66.3%	23.1%	56.0%	18.3%
Impact on academic performance	65.0%	31.1%	52.9%	16.9%	67.7%	24.2%	60.0%	20.7%
School and classroom climate								
Indirect effects on classroom climate	68.3%	23.9%	54.0%	13.4%	66.1%	20.6%	66.0%	19.6%
Indirect effects on students due to concerns for their peers	67.7%	31.0%	58.0%	13.0%	70.7%	21.1%	66.7%	19.8%
Increased bullying	41.0%	25.2%	34.4%	19.8%	37.3%	22.2%	37.7%	27.2%
Parental involvement								
Parents expressing concerns at school	60.7%	35.1%	40.6%	21.5%	50.9%	32.3%	50.6%	27.6%
Decreased parent involvement	53.1%	29.0%	37.0%	15.4%	53.2%	29.4%	42.7%	24.3%

Source: The immigration enforcement survey data.

* Respondents perceived the impact as being "a lot" or "extensive."

on students due to concerns for their friends were reported at a similar level (67–71 percent) by educators from all regions other than the Midwest (58 percent). Over 30 percent of northeastern educators, in particular, noticed this impact to be "extensive," which was 19 percentage points higher than the share of midwestern educators who witnessed the same problem. Educators in northeastern schools also tended to report increased bullying to a degree that was similar to or more frequent than their counterparts in the South. For example, northeastern educators reported heightened bullying at levels higher than the other three regions.

Parents were also affected by ramped-up immigration enforcement activities. Of the respondents in the survey, northeastern educators were more likely to report parents expressing concerns to school personnel than respondents from the other three regions. Compared to southern educators, in particular, the share of northeastern educators who reported this issue was higher by 20 percentage points. We speculate that this may be due to the northeastern parents feeling safer than southern parents communicating their concerns to school staff. Declining parental involvement was also commonly reported by the respondents in our data. Yet again, more than a half of southern and northeastern educators reported this problem, with close to 30 percent ranking it as "extensive." Again, this could be interpreted as parents being less trusting of the schools or more fearful of appearing in public, but the results presented here are not meant to generalize to an entire region. Rather, these results suggest that state-level policies and attitudes regarding immigration enforcement may be less salient than local policies and practices. We test this hypothesis with an analysis of impact by local context described in the next section.

Differing Levels of Impact on Schools by Political Landscape

Our initial hypothesis was that educators in red states with conservative attitudes about immigration would report a greater impact on students and schools. However, as we probed the data to identify regional trends, we found that federal- or state-level policies may affect local communities differently. This became evident in additional interviews with administrators and practitioners that are discussed in chapter 7.

Schools in the West, for example, reported relatively less-extensive im-pacts than other regions, although the impacts observed in western schools were not insignificant. We sampled districts in three western states, and it is noteworthy that the majority of our data for the West region came from California educators, as it is the most populous state, with several geographically and politically distinctive regions. The relatively less harsh impact reported by educators in western schools may indicate that Cali-fornia's statewide efforts—to protect immigrants by designating the state a sanctuary and districts and schools as safe havens—have been at least some-what effective. In short, a relatively favorable attitude toward immigrants in the western states could be a reason for the somewhat mitigated impacts of immigration enforcement reported by educators in the West.

Nevertheless, state-level analyses reveal some other interesting findings. As table 2.5 shows, we compared two southern states (Texas and Tennessee) and one western state (Oregon) with California. Note that although we refer to four states in this section, we acknowledge the limited coverage of schools in our data for each state. Hence, the analysis we conducted is not intended to be a state-level comparison, rather it points up the variation by local context even where states may share similar political leanings. Texas and Tennessee are politically conservative states overall, where support for the Trump administration's immigration policies has been comparatively high. Nonetheless, the results for Texas were much more similar to those for California schools than for Tennessee schools. In some respects, such as school and classroom climate (indirect effects on the classroom and on other students, and bullying), the results for the Texas schools showed a lower degree of impact than California schools, where the state overall is more protective of immigrant households. In contrast to the Texas-California comparison, the results for Oregon, despite its supportive position for im-migrants in general, were similar to, or even worse, than the results for Tennessee. On almost all behaviors the survey explored, a higher share of educators in Oregon schools reported observing these behaviors than their counterparts in the three other states. Taken together, this suggests that local political context may be more important than state or regional context. We revisit this issue in chapter 7.

TABLE 2.5   Impacts of immigration enforcement by political landscape

	ALL	CALIFORNIA	OREGON	TEXAS	TENNESSEE
Psychosocial stress					
Students expressing concerns and fears at school	84.5%	84.8%	91.5%	81.2%	90.0%
Increased behavioral and/or emotional problems	79.6%	79.0%	88.7%	76.2%	83.5%
Academic challenges					
Increased absenteeism	58.3%	53.6%	72.5%	50.7%	71.4%
Impact on academic performance	61.4%	58.6%	74.6%	59.9%	69.9%
School and classroom climate					
Indirect effects on classroom climate	64.9%	65.1%	81.2%	59.1%	71.8%
Indirect effects on students due to concerns for their peers	66.7%	65.8%	81.9%	62.0%	77.7%
Increased bullying	37.6%	35.8%	58.1%	34.9%	43.1%
Parental involvement					
Parents expressing concerns at school	50.5%	51.1%	64.1%	52.1%	61.0%
Decreased parent involvement	45.3%	41.4%	56.4%	49.2%	57.4%

Source: The immigration survey data.

Impact on Urban Versus Suburban Schools

We also examined differences between urban and suburban schools. Urban schools, it appeared, were more acutely affected by increasing immigration enforcement than suburban schools. Given that many immigrant populations are concentrated in urban areas, these results are not startling, but neither was this a foregone conclusion. One could speculate that the impacts may be greater in schools where immigrant students and parents stand out as different from the majority of other students and their families. Sometimes there is safety in numbers.

As table 2.6 demonstrates, urban school educators were more likely than their counterparts in suburban schools to observe negative changes in their students' and parents' behaviors. In some cases, the difference in responses between urban and suburban schools was ten percentage points. Not only were the impacts notable in urban schools, the share of respondents perceiving the effects as "extensive" was also significantly higher among educators in urban schools than suburban ones. Beyond the very high percentage of both urban and suburban educators who reported observing psychosocial

TABLE 2.6   Impacts of immigration enforcement reported by urban and suburban school educators

	URBAN		SUBURBAN	
	Observed	Extensive*	Observed	Extensive
Psychosocial stress				
Students expressing concerns and fears at school	86.3%	46.6%	81.6%	41.1%
Increased behavioral and/or emotional problems	82.5%	35.1%	76.1%	28.7%
Academic challenges				
Increased absenteeism	60.7%	21.2%	55.5%	18.0%
Impact on academic performance	64.9%	24.2%	57.6%	22.1%
School and classroom climate				
Indirect effects on classroom climate	67.9%	21.6%	60.6%	17.6%
Indirect effects on students due to concerns for their peers	70.0%	23.3%	61.8%	16.4%
Increased bullying	39.2%	27.7%	34.8%	24.1%
Parental involvement				
Parents expressing concerns at school	53.9%	30.6%	43.9%	23.9%
Decreased parent involvement	47.5%	25.0%	42.8%	25.9%

Source: The immigration survey data.
*Respondents perceived the impact as being "a lot" or "extensive."

stress in their immigrant students (86 percent and 82 percent, respectively), nearly seven of ten urban educators reported indirect effects on classroom climate and on classmates.

Immigration issues that affect schools are not just urban and suburban phenomena, as there are significant numbers of immigrant workers and their families living in rural areas. Specifically, the share of immigrants in US rural areas is 4 percent, while the share of immigrants in urban areas is 22 percent and 11 percent in suburban areas.[10] This may be a considerable undercount as undocumented persons are reluctant to respond to census counts and many move frequently and are not permanent residents, especially where families follow crops or short-term jobs. Although relatively small in numbers, immigrants contribute substantially to rural communities by participating as an essential part of the rural economy, including in agriculture, construction, meatpacking, and manufacturing industries.[11] Nevertheless, since the majority of immigrants reside in large metro areas, and we focused on areas with high immigrant numbers, we were less able to survey educators in rural areas.[12] However, we were able to interview a number of education leaders from rural areas, which we discuss in chapter 7.

HOW ARE SCHOOL CHARACTERISTICS RELATED TO THE OVERALL IMPACT OF IMMIGRATION ENFORCEMENT?

The questions we posed earlier in this chapter explore the extent to which the impacts of immigration enforcement are associated with school characteristics, such as student demographics, educators' roles, and geographic and political context. As explained earlier (in the section, "How We Examined the Data"), we sought to determine what we call the "comprehensive or overall impact." To do that, we pooled responses for the nine questions (students' expression of concerns and fears, behavioral and/or emotional problems, absenteeism, etc.), generated a variable that reflects an average score of all nine responses, and then combined this average score with the different school-level characteristics (from NCES data). We ultimately discerned that, although the impacts across the nation are far-reaching, the *degree* to which schools are impacted can be linked to several of these characteristics.

Relationships Between the Overall Impact and School Demographics

As figure 2.3 illustrates, in looking at the percentages of White, Black, Asian, and ELL students, the more the dot is placed to the right, the stronger the variable is associated with the overall impact of immigration enforcement.

In examining school demographics, for example, we discovered that when more White students are enrolled in school, educators are more likely to observe negative changes as a result of immigration enforcement. The White share of students was associated with the overall impact in a significant way. Unlike the White share, the percentages of Black and Asian students were not significantly linked with the overall impact. Another salient factor in predicting the overall impact of immigration enforcement was the share of ELLs in school, which can also be a good proxy for children of

FIGURE 2.3 Overall impacts of immigration enforcement

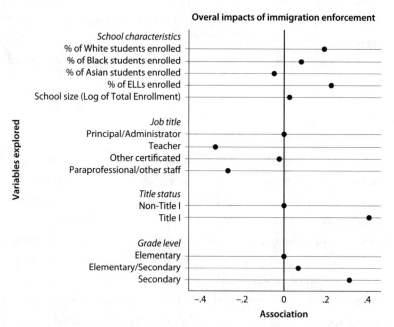

Note: Dots in the figure represent a magnitude (or coefficient) showing the extent to which the variable is associated with the overall impacts of immigration enforcement. The dots on the right side of the x = 0 baseline are, for example, more strongly associated with the impact of immigration enforcement, after holding the other variables in the model constant. Variables used for this analysis are standardized to put different variables on the same scale with a mean of 0 and a standard deviation of 1. The x = 0 baseline represents the standardized mean of the result.

immigrants. ELLs are overwhelmingly born in the United States. However, given that they are usually from immigrant families, it is highly probable that the larger the percentage of ELLs enrolled, the more likely educators are to observe a higher level of negative impact because their families are likely targets of enforcement.

Varying Frequency of Observations by Educator Role

As shown in figure 2.3, school principals, administrators, and other certificated educators, including school counselors and psychologists, tended to report adverse changes among students and parents owing to immigration enforcement activity to a greater degree than teachers. The difference was also statistically significant. Administrators were also somewhat more likely than counselors or other certificated personnel to report these negative effects, though not to a level of statistical significance. It is worth mentioning, though, that counselors were the most descriptive of the educators in relaying the actual experiences and comments of the students (see chapter 4). We surmise that these differences resulted from the different roles and responsibilities of the educators. Those in leadership roles oversee the entire community beyond one classroom; school counselors and psychologists work with students schoolwide, and their job often entails listening to the challenges that students are facing. Teachers, however, may or may not have immigrant students in their classrooms and, in any case, often have a smaller sample of these students and, especially at the secondary level, less time to observe them.

Differences in Observations Reported by Elementary and Secondary Educators

Are students in different grade levels affected differently by aggressive immigration enforcement? Secondary school educators were more likely to perceive the impacts of immigration enforcement than their counterparts in elementary schools (see the figure) and was highly significant. Older students may be more likely to acknowledge to their teachers and other school personnel the disruption in their lives and the lives of their parents, siblings, relatives, friends, or neighbors. Parents may also talk more openly to their older children to prepare them for difficult situations, including where their child should live and how to take care of younger ones in case they are deported. Parents may withhold these difficult topics from conversations with younger children so as not to frighten them. Younger children may also be less expressive about their fears.[13] Thus, educators working with younger students may not perceive the same level of impact that secondary educators do. Nonetheless, as chapter 4 describes, many very young children communicated heartbreaking stories of their family's dire circumstances, including concerns about a parent's detention and deportation as well as losing a job because of ICE raids.

Finally, another notable finding is the stark differences in reporting between Title I and non–Title I educators. Given that most immigrant children are enrolled in Title I schools and the unique challenges these school face, we continue our discussion of the Title I context in the next chapter.

CONCLUSION

In this chapter, we examined educators' responses to the impact of increasingly aggressive immigration policies under the Trump administration on their school community and focused on four questions: (1) how do educators across the nation perceive the effects of immigration enforcement?; (2) to what extent does the impact vary by location (e.g., region, urbanicity, and political landscape)?; (3) to what degree are the effects linked to school demographic composition?; and (4) to what extent does the role and school grade level of the educators impact their observations?

With respect to the first question, an alarming 85 percent of educators observed "students expressing concerns and fears at school," with students worrying about potential deportations of their parents or siblings, or their own deportation, and fearful about their parents losing jobs that sustained the household. Eighty percent of survey respondents noted an increase in "students' behavioral and/or emotional problems," including students' shutting down, coming to school crying, not engaging in class, refusing to eat, and even attempting suicide. Nearly 60 percent of educators observed "increased absenteeism," and more than 60 percent of respondents reported an "impact on the academic performance" of their students. Two in three educators in the survey reported "indirect effects on the classroom climate" and "indirect effects on students due to concerns for their peers" from immigrant families. Moreover, close to 40 percent of respondents reported "increased bullying" of immigrant students. These high percentages portray the widespread disruption experienced by students and schools in all regions.

Although similar reaction patterns emerged across the four census regions in the survey, some regional variations were noteworthy. Southern and northeastern educators' responses stood out, in particular, compared to responses from western and midwestern educators. It was also evident that urban schools generally were hit harder by enforcement activities than suburban schools were. Nevertheless, our state-level comparisons also showed that the level of impact reported by educators varied depending on local contexts, regardless of the presumed political landscape of a community. Although our survey did not examine what contributed to such varying levels of impacts on different communities, interviews with local organizations and education leaders revealed that collaborations with community organizations and NGOs were clearly a factor that we discuss in chapter 7.

As for potential associations between the overall impact of immigration enforcement and school-level characteristics, we discovered that these impacts were more associated with the shares of White students and ELLs than other student groups. The share of White students was most prominent when we focused specifically on the issue of bullying. The frequency of observations by job title also varied. Educators in the leadership positions, with a broader view of the whole campus, tended to observe an adverse impact on students and their families more frequently than teachers. The grade level of school also mattered. Educators in secondary schools were more likely to report impacts on students than elementary school educators.

In spite of variations by region, educators' roles in school and the grade levels of school, there was nearly unanimous agreement that schools or districts should address immigration concerns by sponsoring community "know your rights" discussions, but these were not happening nearly enough. The impact of immigration enforcement is not confined to particular immigrant students and often indirectly impacts their nonimmigrant peers. Broad anxiety and concerns often permeate the whole classroom and school community, making both teaching and learning more challenging. As evidenced by the survey results summarized in this chapter, stepped-up immigration enforcement, reinforced by anti-immigrant rhetoric from the White House, has contributed to a hostile environment where students experience bullying both in and outside of school. Rather than placing the burden of addressing these issues on individual teachers, schools and districts would be wise to create strategies and solutions to overcome these various challenges by involving local stakeholders and by providing educators with resources, such as psychologists, social workers, and legal experts. We discuss these school- and district-level efforts in chapter 7 and conclude with a set of recommendations in chapter 9.

Survey Instrument

**PERCEPTIONS OF THE IMPACT OF IMMIGRATION ENFORCEMENT
ACTIVITIES ON SCHOOLS**

1. Have you observed any students in your classroom or your school who are concerned about immigration issues that may be affecting them, their families, or people they know?
2. Have you noticed any increase in absences that may be related to concerns about immigration enforcement?
3. Have you noticed any behavioral and/or emotional problems with any of your students that appear to be related to concerns about immigration enforcement?
4. Have you noticed a decline in student academic performance that may be related to concerns about immigration issues?
5. Have any of your students expressed any concerns or fears about immigration enforcement?
6. [An open-ended question] What concerns have students expressed?
7. Are concerns about immigration enforcement impacting any of your students indirectly by affecting classroom climate?
8. Are concerns about immigration enforcement affecting any of your students indirectly because of their concern for fellow students?
9. Have any parents of students expressed any concerns to you about immigration issues or enforcement?
10. Have you noticed any decline in parent involvement in your school that appears to be related to concerns about immigration enforcement?
11. Have you noticed any increase in bullying (verbal or physical) related to the perceived immigration status of students or their parents over the last year?
12. Do you think it is necessary to discuss immigration issues at the school-community level?

13. Have you attempted to discuss immigration issues and how to respond to immigration agents with students and/or parents?
14. Has your school attempted to discuss immigration issues and how to respond to immigration agents with students and/or parents?

INFORMATION ABOUT EDUCATORS AND THEIR SCHOOLS

Please select the answer that best describes your role at the school.

1. At what grade(s) or school level do you work?
2. What percent of students in your school do you estimate come from immigrant homes?
3. Please select the name of your school. Your responses to this survey will be kept confidential and NEVER matched with the school name. The name of your schools will be used only for verifying the integrity of our research sample.

(Optional) If you would like to be interviewed on this topic, please provide your email address.

*Response scales:

Q1:	☐ Yes	☐ No	☐ I don't know		
Qs 2–11 (except Q6):	☐ No	☐ A little	☐ Somewhat	☐ A lot	☐ Extensive (Likert scale)
Qs 12–14:	☐ Yes	☐ No			

CHAPTER 3

Immigrant Students and Title I Schools in a Period of Pandemic

A Perfect Storm

JONGYEON EE AND PATRICIA GÁNDARA

T HE MOST CONSPICUOUS change in American schools for the past several
decades is a dramatic increase in immigrant students. The immigrant
population has more than doubled from 8.1 million in 1990 to 18 million
in 2018, an upturn estimated to account for about one-fourth of the US
school-aged students in 2018.[1] As discussed in chapter 1, the increase in
immigrant students since the 1970s is, in part, due to immigration policies
that have made it much more difficult for workers to move back and forth
across the US-Mexico border. With few or no legal options for workers to
enter the country and increasingly harsh border control, many otherwise
seasonal workers choose to stay north of the border with their families,
rather than risk the dangerous trip to reunite with their families in their
country of origin.[2] In addition to bolstering the declining birth rate in the
United States, immigrant students bring many assets with them. Latino
immigrants and many others bring another world language, while all bring
important multicultural perspectives, resilience and tenacity, and as has

been noted in a number of studies, an optimism that can be less evident in many native-born students.[3] At the same time, immigrants also have significant challenges.

Nearly half (47 percent) of Latino children of immigrants live at or near poverty, and an additional 12 percent live in deep poverty, less than half of the official poverty line, which means these households lack the basic necessities of life.[4] This is especially true for children of undocumented immigrants where employment can be tenuous and underpaid. Immigrant students also struggle disproportionately with numerous obstacles associated with poverty, including food insecurity, unstable housing and forced residential mobility, lack of access to medical care, and limited access to early childhood education programs because of language and cultural barriers, immigration status, and discrimination. Up to 30 percent of Mexican immigrant families are reported to suffer food insecurity, and this is only made worse by local law enforcement partnerships such as those discussed in chapter 5.[5] Generally speaking, multiple residential moves are associated with a myriad of educational problems, including declining grades, disciplinary problems, and being held back in school, and this is especially true for low-income students.[6] Immigrant students are more inclined to move than other students because of the instability of jobs and the frequent need to move for employment, as well as the search for more affordable housing. This can be particularly disruptive of schooling for the children of immigrants, in good part because their social networks are frayed, they are unknown to their teachers, and they lack support systems as they move from place to place.[7]

While most children of immigrants are US-born and qualify for federal health insurance, known as the Children's Health Insurance Program (CHIP), those who are foreign-born, including DACA holders, do not qualify for this benefit. Moreover, while one-fourth of children in the United States are Latino, almost 40 percent (39.5 percent) of all uninsured children are Latino. This includes the relatively small percentage who are ineligible because of immigration status. As researchers at Georgetown University point out, "[T]he relentless efforts by the Trump administration to . . . target immigrant communities has impacted our nation's most vulnerable children."[8] Researchers report that increasing numbers of the children of immigrants, even those students who qualify for health-care benefits, are forgoing needed health care because of immigration policies, such as the threat of the "public charge" rule, which could cause them to lose or become ineligible for legal status.[9] Of course, it hardly needs mention that children who are sick, have painful dental problems, or cannot see the board or printed page are not in a state to concentrate fully on learning.

Immigrant and Latino children are significantly less likely than other students to have attended preschool, which is critically important for narrowing initial achievement gaps.[10] These students are also likely to have parents who have little to no familiarity with the US school system and are, therefore, unable to help their children navigate the schools or be of much assistance with homework. Sometimes fearful of going to the school or talking with educators, whom they see as representatives of government, some immigrant parents forgo the opportunity to communicate with teachers about their children's needs. Many of these students are ELLs), at least initially upon entering school. Since English is the language of the classroom in most US schools, this is a significant disadvantage for ELLs, who consistently have the lowest academic test scores of all demographic groups except special education students.[11] A large body of research supports the fact that educational outcomes for ELL students are superior for bilingual education (including college going) over English-only instructional models, but such programs are in short supply, in part because they are sometimes viewed as "coddling" immigrant students.[12]

These same immigrant children are disproportionately enrolled in Title I schools, where most will be segregated with other students like themselves with significant challenges and very limited resources. It is widely acknowledged that although Title I schools are charged with eliminating the opportunity gaps for the most socially and economically disadvantaged students in our society, they lack the resources to actually do the job.[13] These early social and educational disadvantages also tend to result in continuing achievement gaps, so that poor and immigrant students can rarely catch up throughout the school years. Such barriers experienced by immigrant students in Title I schools are easily exacerbated in the face of intensified immigration enforcement. The Trump administration's stringent immigration policies created additional roadblocks that, in effect, made it increasingly challenging for high-poverty schools with many immigrant students to narrow chronic achievement gaps. In fact, the evidence suggests that the gaps are widening.[14]

With these concerns in mind, this chapter provides a concise overview of the federal Title I program, considering the special challenges Title I schools face, and then examines the impact of immigration enforcement on some of these Title I schools compared to others across the country. We first briefly explore the history and context of Title I, the role and effectiveness of federal support, as well as the challenges these schools face. We also investigate a deep association between high-poverty schools and the immigrant student population. We next present results about the extent to which Title I schools were affected by the Trump administration's immigration enforcement policies. Finally, we consider the special impact of the coronavirus pandemic, creating a perfect storm for immigrant students when combined with immigration enforcement.

TITLE I AND THE ROLE OF THE FEDERAL GOVERNMENT IN THE SCHOOLING OF IMMIGRANT STUDENTS

The Elementary and Secondary Education Act (ESEA) of 1965, one of the planks of President Lyndon Johnson's War on Poverty, marked the first substantive involvement of the federal government into American education. Because the Constitution leaves the role of education to the states, the ESEA was constructed to support the states, but not usurp their power over educational decisions. Over time, however, each reauthorization of the ESEA has inched a little closer to being prescriptive. Title I, in particular, is the primary pillar of the ESEA program and has the largest budget ($15.8 billion), accounting for 40 percent of federal spending on K–12 education as of 2019.[15] Although its budget is only 4.6 percent of Title I, Title III is another federal program that supports the education of ELLs, who are almost always the children of immigrants.[16] Title III replaced the 1968 Bilingual Education Act in 2001 with funding more specifically tailored to English acquisition than bilingual instruction. However, the latest iteration of the ESEA passed in 2015, Every Student Succeeds Act (ESSA), is relatively silent on the language(s) of instruction. The federal share of education funding has never reached even 10 percent of states' total education budgets (and currently stands at just over 8 percent).[17]

The primary means by which the federal government attempts to hold educators accountable in Title I and Title III programs and advance its goal of increasing educational opportunities for economically disadvantaged students and ELLs is through statewide testing.[18] High-stakes (states *can* lose funding) standardized testing has been broadly criticized for reducing the curriculum in poor schools to little more than test prep and eliminating the teaching of anything that isn't on the test, resulting in an impoverished curriculum.[19] Nonetheless, the US Department of Education views standardized testing as a useful tool to gauge the effectiveness of the Title I and Title III programs.

Under this federal education policy and funding system—particularly since the No Child Left Behind era (the ESEA reauthorization of 2001)—schools and districts receiving Title I funds are subject to annual evaluations. Since 2015 (under ESSA), schools are held accountable in reaching proficiency targets through a state's standardized assessment system. Title III schools, under this rigorous accountability system heavily dependent on tests, are responsible for demonstrating their ELL students' academic progress annually in order to receive Title III grants. The framework also specifies the time period in which students must make demonstrable progress in achieving English proficiency, keeping pressure on teachers to meet these timelines. Specifically, schools and districts must show measurable improvement not only on ELL students' English proficiency, but also on their performance regarding academic subjects, including math, English language arts, and sometimes science.[20] In this context, which is again governed by reporting requirements based on high-stakes standardized testing, the funding structures of Title I and Title III are closely intertwined.

While there have been many attempts by the federal government to evaluate the effectiveness of the Title I program, there is no definitive answer to the question of its effectiveness. The federal government does not specify exactly how funds are to be distributed at the district level or for what the funds can be used; thus enormous variation in funding and expenditures from district to district and school to school makes drawing hard conclusions impossible. Nonetheless, Elizabeth Cascio and Sarah Reber claim that although Title I has slightly decreased the gap in school spending over time, particularly between richer and poor states, the effect is not readily observable because the amount of money itself is insufficient to reduce the gap substantially.[21] However, if schools do not show progress on test scores, they can be deemed as failing schools and come under the conservatorship of the state. Notwithstanding the limited impact of Title I funds (and to a lesser extent, Title III), they are critical for these high-need, low-income schools and their students. The threat of pulling funding or being reorganized under different leadership for failure to meet testing goals keeps enormous pressure on these schools.

The 1964 Civil Rights Act contained a provision to commission a study of *Equality of Educational Opportunity,* to be delivered to the Congress in July 1966, a year after the passage of the ESEA. This came to be known as the landmark Coleman Report.[22] The national study, which was overseen by James Coleman, then a professor at Johns Hopkins University, found deeply segregated and unequal schools across the nation in which the two most important elements affecting student outcomes—the quality of the teaching staff and the composition of peers—were very unequally distributed. "Minority" (principally Black) students were taught in segregated schools by less-well-prepared teachers, and their classmates' home resources (e.g., parental education, books in the home) were much more limited, as were their aspirations, than those of White students in segregated White schools.[23] The report also found, importantly, that White students were less affected by the quality of their schools than were minority pupils, who evidently relied more heavily on their schools for dedicated instruction. The Coleman Report was prescient in that it described a situation in the mid-1960s that continues today: teacher quality and the segregation of poor and "minority" students remain two of the most vexing challenges for Title I schools. Moreover, we have seen—and will discuss later—that students from low-income backgrounds, and especially immigrant children, have been disproportionately affected by the closure of schools and reduced instruction caused by the coronavirus pandemic.

More than fifty years later, the same conditions noted in the Coleman Report are entrenched. One thing, however, has changed: a growing understanding that schools alone cannot fully make up for the forces in the homes and neighborhoods that counter educational success, such as the conditions of devastating poverty, neighborhood and school segregation, and as we have described, immigrant students' fear of ICE agents. While desegregation battles were fought in the courts, Title I could at least commit funds to support the states in strengthening the schooling experience for poor and minority students. Thus, bettering the lives of the poor through quality public education was a central idea of the Johnson administration's War on Poverty and set the agenda for Title I.[24]

Challenges Faced by Title I Schools

Title I schools are characterized by extreme segregation in race and ethnicity, by poverty, and sometimes by language as well.[25] In this mix are immigrant families, some who are undocumented or with mixed immigration status, and a disproportionate number of students who are in the process of learning English (current or former ELLs). It is also critical to understand the lack of fairness in the way that most states fund their schools. Since most states support their schools at least partially through local property taxes, schools in poor communities often receive less funding because they generate lower taxes. The funds provided by Title I do not come close to equalizing per pupil spending between Title I and more affluent schools. In other words, the schools that have the greatest needs receive the least funding.

A large body of research has reported on the many issues these schools tackle. First, teacher shortages in high-poverty schools are a typical problem that worsens the quality of instruction in Title I schools.[26] In fact, frequent teacher or administrator turnover and high attrition rates are a chronic issue that more acutely affects impoverished public schools across the nation. Specifically, many Title I schools struggle to hire new teachers and retain qualified veteran teachers due to poor working conditions, lower salaries, larger classes, and more problems related to school, neighborhood, and community safety. Of course, such shortages of qualified faculty affect students and the teachers who remain in the school and eventually the education system in general.

Added to the revolving door of teaching staff and inadequate financial resources, the curricula Title I schools offer are far less rigorous compared to more affluent non–Title I schools.[27] Moreover, special programs that engage students in quality educational experiences (e.g., leadership, performing arts, foreign language, advanced mathematics and science programs, Advanced Placement) are often unavailable or not as comprehensive as the ones available in more affluent schools.[28] Not only are the basic courses required for college admission sometimes not available in these high schools, but students also often suffer from teachers' lower expectations and instruction less tailored for college-going plans, severely limiting students' horizons.[29] The lack of financial and human resources as well as a less rigorous academic climate in Title I schools are negatively reflected in numerous academic outcomes, including academic underachievement, chronic absenteeism, and high dropout rates, particularly for minority students.[30`]

As noted in the Coleman Report, segregation also continues to be a very significant problem for Title I schools. Although the schools do not collect data on individual students' immigration status, the Organization for Economic Cooperation and Development (OECD), to which the United States belongs, does collect information on students from immigrant households through its Program for International Student Assessment (PISA) on thirty-seven countries around the world. In a recent OECD study, the organization found that two-thirds of fifteen-year-old students from immigrant homes in the United States were clustered in schools in which at least half of students were also from immigrant homes. The study makes the point that while these students perform poorly on academic tests, it is not because they are educated with other immigrant students; rather it is due to the fact that these immigrant students are socioeconomically disadvantaged.[31]

Similarly, the Civil Rights Project at UCLA recently completed a study showing that the typical Latino student attends a school in which more than half of the other students are Latino, although Latinos represent only a quarter of all students in the general population, and this segregation is typically accompanied by high percentages of poor students.[32]

DOUBLE HURDLES: ELLS IN HIGH-POVERTY SCHOOLS

Although it is widely known that an overwhelming number of immigrant students attend high-poverty schools, specific statistics regarding the actual numbers enrolled, their poverty levels, and their race rarely exist. Given that schools cannot collect or release information regarding the immigration status of students or parents, ELL data are a reasonable proxy for students who are immigrants or who come from immigrant households. Thus, we delve into the ELL population to understand the relationships between ELLs and their representation in poverty schools. This issue is critically important because ELL students require additional resources, above and beyond other low-income students, and their teachers require additional training and skills to adequately educate them. Students need curriculum materials to assist their transition to English or to biliteracy, and teachers need ongoing professional development.[33] Title III funds can be used to pay for some of these material needs, but Title III funds do not address the hardships caused by immigration enforcement or the constant need to retrain teachers for these students because of teacher turnover.

The population of ELLs has grown continuously over the past decades. American public schools had 3.8 million ELLs in fall 2000; since then, this population has grown by over 30 percent. In fall 2017, 5 million ELLs attended schools across the nation, accounting for 10.1 percent of the US public-school student population, with 16 percent beginning school in kindergarten or first grade as ELLs.[34] A large majority of ELL students (75 percent) speak Spanish as their home language, and the rest are from various language backgrounds, including Arabic, Chinese, Vietnamese, and Somali, to name a few.[35] In terms of race and ethnicity, 76.5 percent of ELLs were Hispanic, and Asian students accounted for 10.7 percent of ELLs. White and Black students represented 6.6 percent and 4.3 percent of the total ELL population, respectively.[36] Native American ELLs were less than 1 percent of the total ELL count. (See figure 3.1.)

To what extent are ELLs found in different types of poverty schools? To investigate this question, we group schools into four categories, used by the National Center for Education Statistics and based on the share of students who are eligible for free or reduced-price lunch (FRPL): high-poverty schools, mid-high-poverty schools, mid-low-poverty schools, and low-poverty schools.[37] Our analyses of the 2015 Civil Rights Data Collection data show that 80 percent of Hispanic ELL students were enrolled either in high-poverty schools (56 percent) or in mid-high-poverty

FIGURE 3.1   Percentage of ELLs of each race in school by poverty status

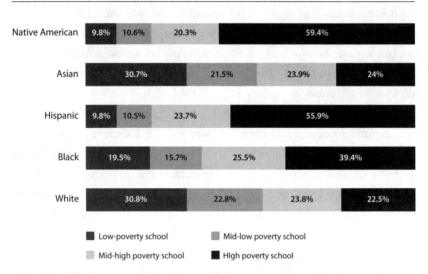

Native American	9.8%	10.6%	20.3%	59.4%
Asian	30.7%	21.5%	23.9%	24%
Hispanic	9.8%	10.5%	23.7%	55.9%
Black	19.5%	15.7%	25.5%	39.4%
White	30.8%	22.8%	23.8%	22.5%

■ Low-poverty school   ▦ Mid-low poverty school
▦ Mid-high poverty school   ■ High poverty school

Source: Civil Rights Data Collection, 2015–2016. ELL counts refer to enrollment of students who are Limited English Proficient (LEP) regardless of students' LEP program enrollment status. High-poverty schools: 75 = < Poverty level = < 100; Mid-high-poverty school: 50 = < Poverty level < 75; Mid-low-poverty schools: 25 = < Poverty level < 50; and low-poverty schools: 0 = < Poverty level < 25

schools (23.7 percent). Only 10 percent of Hispanic ELLs attended low-poverty schools. More specifically, nearly 3 million Hispanic students from immigrant homes across the United States go to either high-poverty or mid-poverty schools. This number is far larger than the combined student enrollment of the three largest US districts: New York, Los Angeles, and Chicago.

IMPACT ON BEHAVIORS OF STUDENTS AND PARENTS BY TITLE I STATUS

We now present findings from the survey of more than 3,600 educators across the nation regarding the impact of immigration enforcement. In table 3.1, we give educators' observations of students and their parents, contrast Title I with non–Title I responses, and illustrate the share of respondents who ranked the impact as being "a lot" or "extensive."

TABLE 3.1   Impacts of immigration enforcement by Title I status

	TITLE I		NON–TITLE I	
	Observed	Extensive†	Observed	Extensive
Psychosocial stress				
Students expressing concerns and fears at school	84.7%	45.3%*	81.3%	31.9%
Increased behavioral and/or emotional problems	79.8%	33.1%*	79.0%	24.9%
Academic challenges				
Increased absenteeism	59.4%*	20.3%*	47.7%	13.8%
Impact on academic performance	61.8%	23.7%	58.0%	18.6%
School and classroom climate				
Indirect effects on classroom climate	64.8%	19.5%	62.0%	21.7%
Indirect effects on students due to concerns for their peers	66.7%	20.1%	63.3%	23.8%
Increased bullying	35.9%*	25.5%	47.2%	30.6%
Parental involvement				
Parents expressing concerns at school	51.2%*	28.5%	36.8%	22.3%
Decreased parent involvement	46.8%*	25.9%	29.8%	18.7%

Source: The immigration enforcement survey data.

Notes: To examine a significant difference between Title I and non–Title I schools, a series of T-tests was conducted for each topic.

* Statistically significant differences emerged between Title I and non–Title I schools.

† Respondents perceived the impact as being "a lot" or "extensive."

Psychosocial (or Socioemotional) Well-being

Among the most important findings, we note first that extremely high percentages of educators in both Title I and non–Title I schools observed the impact of immigration enforcement on students' psychosocial or socioemotional well-being. Two questions in our survey tapped into these indicators of socioemotional well-being: (1) students expressing concerns and fears in the classroom, and (2) students exhibiting behavioral or emotional problems.

The first was generally reflected in students talking about their concerns with others so that educators could observe it. The second consisted of things like being distracted, crying, or having emotional outbursts at school. Over 80 percent of educators in both types of schools noted their students expressed concerns and fears at school, and similar percentages of respondents witnessed an increase in their students' behavioral and emotional problems. No statistically significant differences emerged between the two types of schools, indicating that educators overwhelmingly attested to observing these negative changes in their students' socioemotional well-being regardless of the school's Title I status. Despite these similar levels of observations, however, educators in Title I schools were significantly more likely than their non–Title I school counterparts to interpret those behaviors as extensive, and the differences were highly significant. Of those who noticed students expressing concerns and fears, almost half of Title I school educators ranked the behavior as extensive, compared to less than one-third of non–Title I school educators. Similarly, over one-third of educators in Title I schools indicated that behavioral and emotional problems were extensive, compared to only one-quarter of non–Title I school educators. In other words, the intensity of these emotional reactions was felt significantly more in the Title I schools, although the rate at which they were observed was very similar across the two types. This suggests that the Title I schools were probably more deeply affected by these behavioral issues.

Academic Impact

Two survey questions also tapped into the impact of immigration enforcement on students' academic trajectories: (1) academic performance (principally declining grades), and (2) absenteeism. While fairly high percentages of educators from both Title I and non–Title I schools (62 percent and 58 percent, respectively) reported an impact on students' academic achievement, the difference between the two types of schools was not significant. However, there was a large and statistically significant difference in the observation of absenteeism between Title I and non–Title I schools. Nearly 60 percent of Title I school educators noted this problem, whereas slightly less than half of respondents from non–Title I schools recognized the same issue. Not surprisingly, more Title I school educators perceived increased absenteeism as extensive compared to non–Title I educators, and this difference was also highly significant. The importance of this finding cannot be overstated as absenteeism, and its frequent consequence, leaving school altogether, has profound effects on both students and schools.

As an extensive body of research demonstrates, absenteeism is a significant obstacle that prevents Title I schools from narrowing extensive achievement gaps between lower-income students and their peers from middle-class homes.[38] Chronic absenteeism immediately affects classroom instruction and school climate because teachers need to suspend their planned instruction to revisit previous lessons for those who have missed the class. It can also lead to various negative outcomes, including reduced academic motivation, lower performance and test scores, as well as diminished college and career readiness. Equally important, it can be a precursor of disenrollment. As Thomas Dee and Mark Murphy detail in chapter 5, aggressive immigration enforcement, such as ICE partnerships with police in some counties, can result in expansive and long-term negative effects on schools and communities that are targeted. Their research also shows that the high-poverty communities—where Title I schools are concentrated—are affected by declining Hispanic enrollment over time.

School and Classroom Climate

Three survey questions inquired about behaviors that were viewed as potentially affecting school and classroom climate: (1) indirect effects on classroom climate; (2) indirect effects on peers; and (3) increased bullying. The responses to these questions were both interesting and provocative. Approximately two-thirds of educators reported observing an indirect impact in both Title I and non–Title I schools, with no significant differences between the two. Across both settings, educators tended to interpret this as behaviors that affected other students whose families were not necessarily targets of enforcement, and that affected the general tenor of the school. Educators mentioned things like the sadness and despair students felt for their classmates who were worried or who had disappeared after an ICE raid in the area. And this difference is worth mentioning: some of the schools in our sample had been directly affected by nearby raids, most others had not, but all experienced the fear and worry about what *could* happen.

The issue of bullying was especially interesting. An appreciable share of educators in the survey noted increased bullying in their school. What is noteworthy is that a significantly higher percentage (47 percent) of non–Title I educators than their Title I school counterparts (36 percent) reported these observations. The share of respondents who identified bullying as being extensive was also larger in non–Title I schools than in Title I schools. With the caveat that at least some forms of bullying take place outside the view of educators, we question the absolute accuracy of these responses. In fact, we infer that children from immigrant homes may be more easily targeted in non–Title I schools but may feel safer in the Title I schools because of the larger percentages of students from similarly affected backgrounds.

Parental Engagement

Two survey questions asked about the impact of immigration enforcement on parents' engagement with their children's schools. Those questions were (1) whether parents expressed concerns about enforcement activity to educators, and (2) whether there had been any notable decrease in parent involvement. We did not necessarily expect to see large increases in parental concerns expressed to educators or large declines in engagement because, for a variety of reasons, significant numbers of immigrant parents are not usually visible in the schools. The result of this analysis was somewhat surprising. About half of Title I school educators reported an increase in parents expressing their concerns at school and noted a drop in parental involvement, with more than one-quarter of those respondents judging the impact to be extensive. The relatively high percentage of educators in Title I schools who noted these changes suggests that parents were engaged at a higher level—and felt a higher level of confidence in school staff in the pre–Trump era—than the parents whose children were enrolled in non–Title I schools. The share of respondents in non–Title I schools who witnessed the negative changes was smaller than the percentages reported by Title I school educators, and the difference between the two was statistically significant. This leads us to question if the educators in these Title I schools aren't simply more sensitive and possibly welcoming to these immigrant families.

Schools can be a vital community center for many immigrant parents, the only institution where some feel safe. Sometimes they are the only place parents living in racially and linguistically isolated communities can access information and services (e.g., a nurse or counselor) critical to their children's well-being. If parents become too fearful to come to school, communication with teachers breaks down. Again, a decrease in parental involvement and an increase in fears expressed by parents are serious concerns for all schools, but these issues appear to be more serious in Title I schools, where a majority of students are from families with very limited resources.

THE CORONAVIRUS PANDEMIC OF 2020 AND THE PERFECT STORM

Schools across the nation (and most of the world) closed by March 2020, and students were sent home to learn remotely via computers. Neither teachers nor parents were prepared for this, and the school year effectively came to end. It is impossible to know at this juncture how much the coronavirus pandemic will affect the children of immigrants over the long run. However, there are some early indications that the impact has been disproportionately severe and potentially long lasting for immigrant students. Latinos have been infected by the virus at rates far beyond their representation in the population, while they have also been disproportionately "essential workers."[39] That is, they tend to work in low-wage service industries, such as caregivers in nursing homes, staff in hospitals, clerks in grocery stores, field-workers, and processors in food production. If fortunate enough to have a job, they are unable to be home with their children and many cannot afford childcare, nor can they afford not to go to work. They usually have no sick leave or government unemployment benefits. Thus, many children of essential workers may have had no one at home to help navigate online learning, even if they had computers and internet access, which many do not. A recent survey of 1,400 immigrant parents in California who had participated in the Parent Institute for Quality Education (PIQE) program, which helps immigrant parents navigate the public schools, found that one of five households did not have a computer or other device to connect to distance learning. One-third of parents did not understand the instructions sent home for how to engage in online learning; more than a fourth did not know if their children had completed their homework. While over 80 percent said they had access to the internet, more than half of respondents in the agricultural Central Valley said they had no email address.[40] Moreover, regular access to the internet was not necessarily in the home. Clearly, they were not accustomed to using the internet effectively as a learning or communication tool. It is safe to say that these students' education has been severely interrupted, and it is likely that their achievement gaps have grown larger, especially when compared to peers with parents who are able to stay at home, who speak English, and who have the requisite materials and computer capability to aid their children's learning. But academics may not be the biggest issue.

Mental health professionals warn of serious and potentially long-lasting mental health problems in children and adolescents; they particularly note the problem for low-income and migrant children. Social distancing, lack of contact with peers and extended family, the closure of schools, which destabilizes normal routines, and the reactions of parents who may be under inordinate stress themselves can cause stress and anxiety in children. Without intervention, which is also difficult to access in a pandemic, these feelings can result in mental health crises.[41]

The pandemic also resulted in millions of job losses. Even though many immigrants are essential workers, they are also subject to layoffs due to less demand for some of the services and labor they provide. Without income, the nutrition schools provide can be critical for students, but with schools closed, not all students get this daily nutrition. An April 2020 national survey of food insecurity in America by the Brookings Institution found that one in five mothers of children under twelve reported that their children had insufficient nutrition during the COVID-19 pandemic. This was three times the rate of food insecurity for children during the Great Recession of 2007–2008.[42] Although many undocumented persons are raising the food we all eat, they are ineligible for the Supplemental Nutrition Assistance Program (SNAP), which helps low-income families buy food. And, although their US-citizen children are eligible, many undocumented parents are afraid to claim those benefits, as we see in the next chapter.

Finally, we have heard from many educators across the country who are worried. Students' lack of connection with school, and the frustration and feeling that their education is slipping away from them or will be useless if their family is deported, has combined with the pressing economic needs of their families. Educators agonize that this will drive many immigrant students to give up on school altogether, seriously jeopardizing their futures. Taken together, the normal conditions of life for the children of immigrants, combined with the inadequate resources of the Title I schools that educate them and now a pandemic that struck hardest on Latinos and immigrants has, indeed, created the perfect storm for the millions of students who form this population.

CONCLUSION

In spite of the federal government's decades-long effort to help ensure a fair and quality education for disadvantaged students in Title I schools, the gaps between poverty schools and schools with more resources have been widening over time.[43] Ironically, this federal-level endeavor committed to closing achievement gaps has been undermined by obstacles erected from another agency of the same federal government. As our analyses show, harsh and random immigration enforcement affects all low-income students in Title I schools, regardless of their immigration status. While Title I schools have long suffered from varied challenges that cannot be addressed in a short period of time, the Trump administration's harsh policies were directly affecting many schools across the nation, especially these Title I schools with sizable numbers of immigrant students. Educators in Title I schools were not only more likely to observe such impacts on their students and school community, but also tended to rank these impacts as more extensive. On virtually every aspect of student behavior observable in school (and included in the survey), the immense share of educators reported negative changes that significantly alter students' schooling experiences and academic outcomes in both short and long terms. Given that the ripple effects caused by immigration enforcement have combined with the hugely disproportionate impact of the coronavirus pandemic on these same children of immigrants and their families, we argue that more extensive and far-reaching consequences for students and their communities are to be expected.

CHAPTER 4

In the Voices of the Educators

PATRICIA GÁNDARA AND JONGYEON EE

I N CHAPTER 2, we saw the very high rates that educators reported observing the impact of immigration enforcement on immigrant students. In fact, when we look at the frequency with which educators mention particular words to describe their students' reactions, "fear" and "concerns" are found alongside "deporting," "parents," and "family." It is clear that students' gravest concerns are about family, and as one administrator put it, "They are just thinking, 'Am I going to have a family when I go home today?'" But so far, these are just numbers. An examination of educators' comments brings to life the very real pain of students who are often sad, worried, and overwhelmed by fear—for their parents, for their siblings, for grandparents and other extended family members, and ultimately for themselves and the uncertain future ahead. Educators' comments also elucidated the ways teaching and learning are seriously compromised for these students and their classmates. The word "schools" is also prominent in figure 4.1. We argue that schools play a very important role in the lives of these students, and that schools, too, are profoundly affected by immigration enforcement that fails to take into account the collateral damage inflicted on these students and their educators.

In this chapter, we present some of the responses to the open-ended question in our 2017–2018 national survey: "What concerns have students

FIGURE 4.1   Educators' most repeated keywords

expressed?" Almost 2,700 respondents described the behaviors and comments of their students from immigrant homes. Some were brief and simply reiterated students' fears of losing their parents, others were more extensive and nuanced, and still others were actually profound and even heartbreaking in recounting the experiences of their students. Altogether they paint a portrait of how immigration enforcement alters the experience of schooling, for them and for their classmates. Comments by educators fall into four categories: (1) psychosocial stress, (2) academic challenges, (3) school and classroom climate, and (4) parental engagement with the school.

PSYCHOSOCIAL STRESS

Students in immigrant families spend much of their time in terror, fearing that their family members will be whisked away and there will be nothing they can do about it. Literally many hundreds of educators informed us that their students lived with constant fear of losing their parents and grandparents, of coming home from school and finding them gone. Researchers have found that fear can permeate a community believed to be targeted by ICE, affecting everyone in that community, even students whose parents are not undocumented. This is especially true for other Latino students, as they often feel that all Latinos are targets, regardless of their immigration status.[1] Fear and helplessness are powerful emotions, and the psychological literature is full of studies that show how these emotions undermine individuals' normal functioning, let alone the ability to concentrate in school.[2] For example, neuroscience studies show that exposure to circumstances that produce persistent fear and chronic anxiety can have lifelong consequences by disrupting the developing architecture of the brain.[3] This can set in motion long-term difficulties with learning, social adjustment, and other physical and mental health problems. Because the actual architecture of the brain is impaired, remedying these problems can be very difficult, if not impossible.[4]

The inability to solve an emotionally challenging problem (such as fear of losing a parent) can result in negative cognitive, emotional, and motivational consequences. Students can display what psychologists call "learned helplessness," a state in which they feel depressed, lacking in motivation, and believe they have lost control over their lives.[5] In the case of immigrant students, the family's loss of control over the most basic aspects of their lives often reflects reality. Survey respondents reported that many students were deeply concerned and worried about being left to care for younger siblings on their own if parents were deported. For example, a fourth-grade teacher in the Northeast recounted what one of her students had told her: "[She] told me that her mom is teaching her how to make food and feed her baby sister in case the mom is taken away." A counselor from the Midwest recounted a similar fear that her students have shared: "Students have worried about how to care for their younger siblings after their mother has been deported. They have stated they have 'now become the mother,' at age fourteen."

Sometimes students close down emotionally, as one California educator reported: "A student spoke at a faculty meeting about her fears about the immigration policies of this administration. She said she had shut down literally for months in class because she feared her parents would be deported." Another California high school teacher explained,

> I had one student who came back the day after prom and would not eat or talk to anyone. I finally found out from one of her friends that she came home from prom to find her mom deported and never had the chance to say goodbye or anything. She was suffering but did not know what to do.

Although younger children were generally less likely to express feelings overtly, they too were described as sometimes "shutting down." A second-grade teacher recounted what had happened to one of her students:

> Her father [was] taken by ICE and [she] was terrified to speak during class. After he was allowed to return [home] the mom told us what had happened and I saw a total change in the student. She participated more, smiled more, and her academic performance improved. It was clear she was carrying a big secret and didn't know how to deal with it.

While some students shut down in an attempt to cope with their fears and stress, others act out their fears. An elementary school teacher from Oregon described how fears of being deported caused some of her students to have "frequent stomach aches and trips to the bathroom, as well as decreased energy for learning." A Maryland teacher described the desperate situation of a student whose mother was deported: "We have one student who had attempted to slit her wrists because her family has been separated and she wants to be with her mother. She literally didn't want to live without her mother." Many educators told of students breaking into tears in class. A California elementary school teacher recounted a scene we heard from many others: "I have had parents who arrived late to pick up their kids after school and students were crying, thinking they had been deported. I've had another student have anxiety attacks in class, worried his dad would be deported."

An Oregon educator also reported students "even having fear walking to school or walking home in the afternoon or even seeing someone in a suit and thinking they might be immigration coming to get them or their parents . . . Some families have even had to go to counseling or even taken pills to help."

All of these turbulent emotions, fears, and anxiety have obvious implications for learning, but also for teaching, and we deal with this in chapter 6.

ACADEMIC CHALLENGES

The evidence is powerful that learning is significantly impaired by psychological stress. As Ross Thompson, Distinguished Professor of Psychology at the University of California, Davis, wrote:

[W]hen children are born into a world where resources are scarce and violence is a constant possibility, neurobiological changes make them wary and vigilant, and they are likely to have a hard time controlling their emotions, focusing on tasks, and forming healthy relationships. Unfortunately, these adaptive responses to chronic stress serve them poorly in situations such as school and work, where they must concentrate and cooperate to do well.[6]

While Thompson was not referring specifically to children facing immigration enforcement, it is hard to imagine any greater violence to a child than having a parent suddenly taken away and not knowing where that parent is. It has also been well documented that when a parent (especially the breadwinner) is removed, many immigrant families face hunger and homelessness.[7] Academic persistence among immigrant students can be affected not only by these kinds of stressors, but also by absenteeism and declining motivation due to a loss of hopefulness about their future.

Stress and Fear and Declining Achievement

Stress and fear are pervasive for these students and, as noted above, often interfere with students' ability to attend to schoolwork, which results inevitably in low and declining grades. A high school administrator from Tennessee summed up the situation:

> They are not thinking about college, or the test next week, or what is being taught in the classroom today. They are thinking about their family and whether they will still be a family; whether their family will remain intact.

A middle school teacher from the Midwest described the reaction of her students to a recent immigration raid in the community,

> I noticed those students behaving so differently. They don't sit or stand tall. They do not want to participate in presentations. They do not want to be called. They seem disconnected or uninterested now. In my community's school, it has been almost too sad to describe the change of countenance of these students. I serve in an academically advanced setting where students are selected and good performers.

Many educators commented on the fact that their high school students tended to be very concerned about the welfare of their parents, more so than for themselves. A high school counselor from Nebraska described how her "students worry about their parents' emotional well-being, leading them to become off task in school. Students have significant concerns, causing emotional detriment, and often leading to worse attendance and grades."

Examining the academic toll that intensified immigration enforcement takes on students, Catalina Amuedo-Dorantes and Mary J. Lopez analyzed Current Population Survey (US Census) data between 2000 and 2013 and found that Hispanic students between six and thirteen years old whose parents were likely undocumented had a 14 percent greater chance of repeating a grade than all other students. Moreover, older students between fourteen and seventeen had an 18 percent greater chance of dropping out of school.[8] Because being held back in school has been shown to have a strong relationship to eventually dropping out, these two findings are likely associated.[9]

Absenteeism and Its Ripple Effects

Recent research shows that Hispanic ELLs (aka children of immigrants) have the highest rates of absenteeism and pay the highest price in terms of lower academic achievement associated with absenteeism among all demographic groups.[10] Some educators marvel that students continue to come to school at all and try to do their best under very difficult circumstances. But there was wide agreement among educators in the survey that academic achievement is often impaired by absenteeism; in chapter 2 we saw that most educators reported this as a problem. One New Jersey administrator reported,

> The kids are scared and sometimes they hide for days when there are immigration raids in the area. Some of the students have no food or place to live because the parents do not have a job and they go day by day.

Many educators noted that students stay home because they are afraid their parents will disappear while they are at school and that parents also fear to send their children to school alone. For example, a California teacher reported that "[s]tudents are having trouble getting to school because parents are afraid to allow them on public transit alone." We also heard many stories of high school students who work to help support their families. A Maryland teacher shared that some of her students have confided they are "having to work because mom can't afford to take care of them with her income [now that dad is gone], which is affecting their grades." Regardless of their reasons for being absent, absenteeism has pervasive effects on students' academic outcomes as well as on the school's ability to educate them. Students who miss school fall behind and eventually can no longer catch up. The situation becomes hopeless and many will drop out, with a profoundly negative impact on the rest of their lives. Absenteeism is also disruptive of the classroom. As one Tennessee teacher put it,

> We've had students and families deported at our school in the middle of the school year. It's a fearful experience for students and also very disruptive to their education. It's discouraging and students struggle to find motivation or incentive to keep doing their work . . . and now we have fewer bodies in the class.

Teachers mentioned the pall that falls over the classroom when the desk of a fellow student sits empty, inducing fear in the rest of the students. Another Tennessee high school teacher described the impact on the whole class when one of her students who had been picked up by ICE but released after more than a month: "This understandably had an immense impact on the rest of my students, as well as his empty seat in the classroom confirmed the reality of their fears every day."

Declining Motivation

Many of these students do continue to apply themselves in school, heeding their parents' advice that they take advantage of the opportunity they have to break out of the cycle of poverty and fear.[11] However, a common theme was the large numbers of talented, hardworking students who had excelled in school and were looking forward to college, but saw their dreams cut short. This was especially the case for DACA students who had their status called into question with President Trump's announcement in 2017 that he was ending the Obama-era program. An elementary school counselor from Oregon relayed how some former students, hoping to hang on to their dream of a college degree, returned to ask her for help: "After DACA, there were former students who have been diligently working toward degrees who were in tears and coming back to ask for any kind of guidance they could get for next steps."

And a Southern California counselor explained her dilemma in trying to keep hope alive for her high school students:

> I have been meeting with various students who feel there is no hope for them and are letting their grades slip because they are under so much stress and unsure about the future. I struggle with encouraging them to have faith when I am unsure myself. I don't like misleading my students and I honestly feel because I don't know what will happen I could be giving them false hope. They are unsure that Government will help and assist them and feel they are second-class citizens. It just breaks my heart.

A high school teacher from Oregon shared her heartbreak for students who came to the United States with their parents as children and studied hard:

> I have students who were college bound now questioning if it's worth it because they don't believe they could get a job in their field after graduating. They're worried about financial aid. This is most heartbreaking for students who want to go into public service, and now are thinking about just working to protect their parents.

One cannot help but think of the loss of human talent that occurs as a result of these immigration policies. Students, born in the United States or having lived almost all their lives here, with a desire to make contributions to their community and preparing themselves to do so, have had their aspirations shattered and their goals derailed. It is notable that in 2018 nearly nine thousand DACA holders were themselves teachers, helping to prepare these and other students for a future in this country.[12]

SCHOOL AND CLASSROOM CLIMATE

The National Center on Safe Supportive Learning Environments of the US Department of Education defines a positive school climate as "fostering safety, promoting a supportive academic, disciplinary and physical environment; and encouraging and maintaining respectful, trusting and caring relationships throughout the school community."[13] More succinctly, school and classroom climate typically refers to characteristics such as a sense of safety, belonging, and inconclusiveness—how one is made to feel about oneself at the school. There is increasing evidence that school and classroom climate are also associated with important academic and socioemotional outcomes for students, and this is especially true for students in low-income communities.[14] There is little in the literature, however, about the impact of school climate on children of immigrants, where a hostile climate at school could augur extremely serious consequences for a student. For example, a Houston high school senior, an immigrant with good grades and captain of the soccer team, was bullied by another student. He defended himself by pushing a girl who had thrown a bottle at him and shouted a racial slur; school police intervened. The student was taken to jail and then transferred to a detention center for removal.[15] Reporting an immigrant student (documented or undocumented) for any infraction to school authorities can result in his or her removal or the removal of the student's family, leaving the student homeless or parentless—many immigrant students' worst fear. Hence, a safe school climate, free of bullying, can be critically important for these students.

School Climate and Academic Self-Concept

Many educators commented on the way that school climate and, sometimes by corollary, classroom climate have been affected both by immigration enforcement policies and by the very negative rhetoric about immigrants espoused by President Trump and his supporters. Students interpret this rhetoric as a rejection of them and their families, which makes them feel like they don't belong. A high school teacher from the Northeast recounted the kinds of things he hears from his students, "Students have expressed concerns that they are living in a country that does not want them, does not see them, that wants them gone . . . They are afraid of ICE. They feel they are targets because of their names, their skin color, their accents, their status. They worry they cannot trust anyone."

And an elementary school teacher from the Midwest described the day after the presidential election at her school: "After the presidential election, children were huddled underneath playground equipment, crying. I ask, 'What's the matter?' They say they think that people hate them so they'll have to go away."

An elementary school teacher from California reported that one of her students asked her, "Why does Trump hate Mexicans so much?" Another elementary school teacher from Maryland shared, "My students and their parents have cried when with me. They fear they are not welcome in our school and in our town." The message sent to the students, even very young students, is "you don't belong," "there is something wrong with you and people like you." Even if the school tries to reassure them, a pervasive message of inferiority has been shown to have debilitating psychological effects on students' self-confidence as learners. Abundant research on stereotype threat has established that when students are aware of negative stereotypes about them and their abilities, they will often underperform because of the anxiety produced by fear of confirming the stereotype.[16] Thus, the negative overall climate for immigrants, associated with hurtful rhetoric, finds its way into the school and affects students' feelings of self-worth and self-efficacy, undermining their belief in their own abilities.[17] Research has also found that a negative concept of oneself as a learner can predict negative academic outcomes.[18]

School Climate and Belonging

Sometimes a school climate may not be overtly hostile; rather it is simply uninviting to immigrant students by failing to acknowledge their presence, such as never highlighting their accomplishments, including them in planning for school activities, or sending out notices in their home language.[19] Feeling included, feeling as though one belongs at school, is very important for students' academic motivation.[20] Some researchers have found that this is especially true for Latino students.[21] While we know of no study that confirms this, we speculate that it must be even more true for immigrant students who always question their ability to "fit in." For example, an Arizona elementary school teacher in our study mentioned how her immigrant students wouldn't speak their home language because they were embarrassed or afraid of being identified as coming from an immigrant home, being "different." One element of fitting in and belonging and creating a positive school climate is participation in extracurriculars, like sports, music, clubs—things that bring students together informally around shared interests and where they can exhibit different talents. What we heard from educators was that immigrant students rarely could participate in anything after school because of their deep fears. Parents wanted them home right after school, and the students, who had worried all day if their family members would still be there, were equally anxious to get home. For high school students, many also had a job waiting to help out the family. Thus, a kind of activity that could help build a positive school climate for these students was unavailable to them. For this reason, some researchers have recommended making extracurriculars curricular, that is, ensuring that many of these socially binding activities can take place during the school day.[22]

School Climate and Bullying

Bullying by other students is a major factor in school climate and in making students feel that they don't belong. Many educators reported bullying of immigrant students, although we suspect that the phenomenon is even more prevalent than the surveys indicate. Bullies are often careful not to be caught in the act by teachers. There is considerable empirical evidence that bullying of nonwhite, immigrant, and other students perceived to be different increased during Donald Trump's campaign for the presidency and since. He referred to Mexican immigrants as criminals and rapists, and advocated barring Muslims' entry to the United States. Francis Huang and Dewey Cornell analyzed survey data from more than 150,000 seventh and eighth graders in Virginia, both before and after the election of Donald Trump. They found a statistically significant uptick in bullying in conservative locales supporting Trump compared to more Democratic areas.[23] John Rogers and his team surveyed 1,500 high school educators across the nation to investigate the impact of the political rhetoric from the 2016 presidential election on students' behavior. They found that an increasing number of schools enrolling mostly White students had become more hostile environments for racial or ethnic and religious minorities.[24]

In contrast to those studies, we found bullying occurring in both liberal and conservative areas, although as noted in chapter 2, schools that enrolled more White students tended to report more bullying. A high school administrator in New York City commented that although the school had not witnessed bullying, "students are stressed by the anti-immigrant climate that is currently being promoted. We have had a significant increase in students reporting incidents of verbal and/or physical abuse in public in the past year and a half."

An elementary school administrator from California, considered a deep blue state, offered, "Students [at the school] use 'Go back to your country!' or another variation as a putdown when arguing. Adults in the neighborhood around the school make similar comments from time to time."

While in these two cases, some or all of the bullying occurred outside the school, it nonetheless can be traumatizing to students (especially those who are already afraid that they can be snatched off the street by ICE) and creates a real challenge for schools attempting to create a safe and welcoming climate for their students. Other educators in supposedly pro-immigrant areas reported various anti-immigrant acts in their schools. A middle school teacher in California shared the following: "Some of my students have family members or friends that may get deported, and they are worried and scared about the climate of increasing intolerance and bigotry. There has also been an increase in racist graffiti, vandalism and racial tensions and language on our school campus. I wonder where all this hate comes from?"

An elementary school teacher in Oregon described how in her school, "bullying has arisen that frequently uses immigration status as a target. 'You'll never see your parents again,' 'I'm gonna call so they take you away' and a sharp increase in slurs targeted toward students of color, regardless of their immigration status."

A high school administrator from California added that at her school, "there have been derogatory comments made between students, i.e., 'they are going to build a wall [and] you won't be able to get back.'" Another western administrator expressed the same concern, particularly about young learners: "Even between young children, taunting each other that 'Trump will send you back to your country!' even if the family members are citizens, the child was born here, etc." As these comments indicate, the border wall was a major theme in many educators' comments. Students taunted other students about Trump building a wall to shut them out, and students often mentioned to their teachers and to each other their concerns about the wall that Trump was going to build. Even US citizen students wondered out loud if they would be sent to the other side of the wall or if family members in Mexico would never again be able to cross the wall to visit.

A Climate of Pervasive Fear and Loss of Trust

Although many educators noted that they tried to create a safe and welcoming campus climate, telling students repeatedly that ICE was not allowed on campus and they were safe at school, rumors and comments they overheard at home or in the community still instigated fear in many students. These students worried that at any moment, an ICE agent could appear, either on their way to and from school, or on the campus itself, and snatch them away. A California middle school teacher reported that "some students fear some teachers because they think their teachers are going to report them to ICE." This may not be far-fetched; chapter 6 recounts concerns of some educators worry that some of their colleagues might do just that, so they don't discuss what they know about students' families with others at their school. An Arizona high school teacher stated, "I believe some students think an agent could show up at the classroom door," and a Florida elementary school teacher reported that some of her students did not want to play outside for fear of immigration officers catching them. Moreover, some educators observed trust between students and the school declining. A high school educator from New York noted, "[Students] don't see school as a safe place from the current ICE policies and they don't see the importance of attending and receiving an education."

Even when students feel generally safe at school, many worry that information about them or their families can put their families at risk, so they refuse to share any personal information with the school. This can make it especially hard for counselors who are trying to address students' needs, as one Texas counselor related: "They are already afraid, somewhat, to give address information. Now they do not want to give any information at all about where they are from or where they live. They do not want to talk about their families and some fear being yanked out of class and just sent away."

A high school teacher in California related that some of his students fear being deported "for minor school infractions despite assurances that their school behavior or academic record won't make a difference."

PARENTAL ENGAGEMENT WITH THE SCHOOL

Although parent engagement with schools can take many forms and vary with different demographic groups, it has generally been shown to be a positive factor in student achievement as well as other behavioral outcomes.[25] There is no doubt that when parents have a trusting relationship with teachers, they are more likely to share information that can be very important for a student's learning and general well-being.[26] However, schools often struggle to engage parents who work long hours, do not speak English, and have difficulty getting away from home because of other responsibilities. Immigrant parents can be even more difficult to engage for all these reasons and the additional fears of ICE agents.[27]

We saw in chapter 2 that parent involvement declined during the period of harsh immigration enforcement when our survey was administered. However, the decline was not as significant as for other behaviors in the survey. We assume that the decline was from an already relatively low level since most parents in immigrant communities do not have the leisure time to devote to their children's school and, as educators conveyed, many of these parents have a great fear of encountering immigration authorities when they leave home. A high school teacher in New York shared, "Some of our students' families are afraid to come into our schools because they fear that since the school is run by the government, they will be taken away." An elementary school teacher from Tennessee described the situation at registration: "[W]hen helping with registration, there were many family members and parents who expressed fear when I asked for proof of residence. They thought I wanted proof of citizenship." Many educators reported that parents would not come to the school to fill out forms for free lunch or field trips because they did not want to divulge information about their family and because they were concerned about the "public charge" edict the Trump administration had announced, which could make individuals ineligible for permanent residency if they used any government services.[28] Of course, the food the school provides is sometimes the only regular nutrition students can count on, so this indicates parents' extreme fear of immigration authorities. Educators also reported that many families would not come to school, even for important events like graduation, sometimes fearing that it can be a trap set by immigration officials. A Tennessee school counselor described one mother's conflicting fears:

> The family [had] three students and the mother would not send her children to school for fear of deportation. The school found out because the family was residing with another family whose children were regularly attending school . . . School officials contacted the parents and advised that the children should be in school or risk being reported for truancy.

The mother felt trapped between two competing threats; the counselor added, "The fear in the Hispanic community is not unwarranted!"

The Need to Outreach to Parents

One of our most powerful findings was that almost all educators believed that it was important to reach out to the community to calm their fears and address their concerns, while making clear that the school was a safe place for their children, but relatively few schools or educators had actually done so. Why? Our interviews with teachers, administrators, and organizations that work with the schools gave us some clues as to why this discrepancy exists. School personnel are not well versed in immigration law and don't always know what to say to parents. Not everyone in the school shares the same attitudes toward immigrant families. These Title I schools often feel overwhelmed and lack the human resources to organize meetings and do outreach to the community.

In many communities of color, there is long-standing mistrust between community members and their schools because of a lack of connection between educators who live outside the community, and who do not look like the people who live in the school community, and the residents of those communities. Anthony Bryk and Barbara Schneider describe the critical element of relational trust between the community and school personnel for urban school reform to be successful.[29] The concept is especially relevant to the schools that serve immigrant families. Among immigrants, trust among parents and students and school personnel is critical. Trust is built on respect and cooperation. Parents and community members must be listened to and taken seriously, which can be especially challenging when parents are afraid to voice their concerns.Principals need to support their teachers in reaching out to parents, and everyone must share the same goal: to provide a safe, welcoming, and inclusive place for all students to thrive.

Some schools work diligently to build that trust by reassuring parents and students that they are safe and protected at school, and that the school will never divulge personal information about them to any outside authority. Many schools in our sample had proclaimed themselves "Sanctuary" or "Safe Haven" schools in an attempt to convey a welcoming message to immigrant families. Where that trust exists and the school climate is welcoming, the school can function as an important resource to parents. A Maryland middle school teacher shared that a few of her "students expressed that they came to school sick because it is much safer for their families to receive help from the school's nurse than a clinic or hospital." An elementary school teacher in Oregon noted, "Parents frequently contact a teacher or staff member they trust to share the most recent rumors or events in the neighborhood, seeking assurance and comfort." Nonetheless, even when parents want to be involved, the fear of immigration enforcement can hold them back. A Massachusetts elementary school teacher recounted a student telling her, "[M]y mom can't volunteer anymore because they need her fingerprints and she doesn't have her card" (referring to a green card, which would give her legal residency). Similarly, an elementary teacher from Maryland wrote that the parents of her students were afraid to serve as chaperones or allow their children to go on field trips. As if to underscore the legitimacy of these parents' concerns, a middle school teacher from a western sanctuary state recounted how "[a] student's father was picked up by ICE last year as he was signing permission slips for his daughter to speak in Washington, DC. Students regularly shared stories of ICE raids and fears that it could happen at home or at school despite our reassurance that no one would take them from school."

News of an incident like this travels fast, undermining any trust that has been built between families and schools, and the tenuous bond between immigrant parents and their children's teachers that the research tells us is so important for children's development can be broken irretrievably.

CONCLUSION

What comes across very clearly throughout the nearly 2,700 comments of educators is the way students' lives in the community and at school are shaped by the constant presence of fear. Students are afraid to leave home to come to school for fear of what can happen while they are away. At school, they are anxious, distracted, and often crying, while they worry about their parents, and sometimes themselves, being taken at any moment. Their futures are uncertain, and they perceive immigration agents to be around every corner. Many students tell their teachers, "What's the point of studying if we are just going to be deported?" All this turmoil disrupts schooling for them as well as for their classmates. A recent survey of Texas and Rhode Island high school students by the Migration Policy Institute found that 12 percent of US-born Latinos feared deportation just on the basis of their ethnicity.[30] Educators mention that students ask, "Where is so-and-so? What's going to happen to him/her?" The empty desks are powerful symbols of uncertain futures. But, as one New York teacher says, "[T]hey keep coming to school hoping things will change." These students are overwhelmingly US citizens, traumatized by a situation not of their making and powerless to change it. In the next chapter, Thomas Dee and Mark Murphy explain how collaborations between ICE and local law enforcement add to the challenges for low-income (Title I) schools by frightening communities and disrupting the school enrollments of Hispanic students.

CHAPTER 5

The Impact of Local ICE-Police Partnerships on Students

THOMAS S. DEE AND MARK MURPHY

T HE DESIGN AND enforcement of immigration policy ranks among the most politically contentious issues of our time. In this chapter, we extend our previous scholarship on the impact of federal ICE partnerships with local law enforcement on Hispanic student enrollment to consider their unique impact in low-income areas (i.e., as proxied by the share of Title I schools). While a substantial amount of public attention spotlights immigration enforcement at the border, important policy changes have also focused on the interior enforcement of immigration law. For example, certain local jurisdictions have actively sought to limit cooperation with the federal ICE branch of the Department of Homeland Security (DHS) by becoming "sanctuary" communities. Others have pushed for greater participation in enforcement efforts by voluntarily engaging in ICE partnerships. In the latter communities, deputized local law enforcement officers supplement the efforts of ICE's Enforcement and Removal Operations bureau, which seeks to identify, arrest, and remove undocumented residents in the United States. Through ICE-police partnerships, ICE trains these local officers, who are afforded the authority to enforce federal immigration law under the supervision of ICE officers. These partnerships between local law enforcement and ICE have substantial consequences for students and schools in these communities. Specifically, we find that the ICE-police partnerships have potentially wide-ranging and long-term negative effects on communities and schools that are targeted, especially in communities with high levels of poverty.

In 1996, section 287(g) of the federal Immigration and Nationality Act introduced the opportunity to form these partnerships. Nearly ten years later, local jurisdictions and the DHS began introducing the 287(g) programs. The subsequent adoption of the ICE-police partnerships occurred over three distinct periods (i.e., 2005–2011; 2012–2016; and 2017–the present). The first phase of the policy, occurring during the second term of the George W. Bush administration and the first term of the Obama administration, was associated with the run-up in national security operations that followed 9/11. The second phase of the policy, during the latter part of the Obama administration, occurred as DHS shifted its focus away from interior enforcement efforts for individuals without prior convictions. The reduction in these partnerships under the Obama administration reflected in part the evidence that the programs encouraged racial profiling. The third phase of the policy began with the onset of the Trump administration and is characterized by a sharp growth in the number of ICE-police partnerships and an emphasis on interior enforcement regardless of prior conviction history. In this chapter, we describe each of these policy phases in greater detail.

We also present new evidence on the effect of ICE partnerships during phase one of the policy, when the most robust program and outcome data are available. First, we consider how adoption of an ICE partnership affected the number of immigration detainers issued during phase one. To study this, we rely on a panel of counties that had applied for ICE partnerships at any point through 2011.[1] Our results indicate that ICE partnerships adopted during phase one led to clear and substantial inceases in the number of immigration detainers issued over time for all counties. Importantly, research shows that parental detentions can have serious and long-term negative effects on children.[2] In addition, we observe larger increases in issued immigration detainers in counties with high concentrations of poverty. These results provide new evidence that these partnerships generated a meaningful increase in immigration enforcement and that the impact of these enforcement policies has an empirically relevant intersection with the level of economic opportunity in a community.

This chapter also highlights recent evidence from phase one on the measured enrollment of Hispanic and non-Hispanic students in US public schools.[3] The data used in this recent study, drawn from universe surveys of school enrollment by ethnicity, may provide a more reliable indicator of the demographic impact of these policies than other studies that rely on self-reported, individual surveys. School districts in the United States have strong financial incentives to report all their enrolled students, and aggregated counts are unlikely to put any undocumented students or students residing in mixed-status families at risk. In contrast, individual-level survey data may impose greater risks for individuals and be more susceptible to misreporting.[4] Results generated by evaluating these data, therefore, provide a more reliable barometer of the demographic impact of the ICE partnerships that were enacted during this period. In our recent study, we find that ICE partnerships had large negative effects on Hispanic student enrollment that grew more negative over time.[5] In that study, we did not explore the potentially important heterogeneity in the impact of these ICE partnerships.

In this chapter, we extend our prior results by assessing the impact of an ICE partnership based on poverty status as measured by a school's Title I status under the federal Elementary and Secondary Education Act.[6] Schools classified as being Title I eligible receive federal funding for enrolling low-income students. We define counties that have high concentrations of poverty as those where Title I–eligible schools represent more than 40 percent of schools in the county. When limiting our sample to these counties, we observe even more severely negative effects of the adoption of an ICE partnership on Hispanic student enrollment.

These student enrollment results are not just demographically important; they also suggest large and substantive negative educational effects. Extensive prior research documents the educational harm of reactive student moves or dropout.[7] To the extent that ICE partnerships increase Hispanic student outflow, mitigate Hispanic student inflow, or encourage Hispanic students to drop out while remaining in place, they generate educational costs. Importantly, these costs likely affected many US citizens, since approximately three-fourths of the children of undocumented residents at this time were estimated to be US citizens themselves.[8] In addition to being harmful for students who move, declines in student enrollment affect school funding levels, which may negatively impact the quality of education for students remaining in the adopting location as well. These ICE partnerships also likely cause enhanced trauma for students in adopting jurisdictions.[9] Additionally, these policies are tied to a range of other harmful unintended consequences in public health, housing foreclosures, economic activity, sustainability of local economy (or industry), community policing, and levels of child hunger, and have not been found to have any meaningful effect on crime rates.[10] This body of evidence illustrates the many costs and corresponding lack of clear benefits associated with the community adoption of these ICE partnerships. Nonetheless, many communities in the United States continue to engage in them.

ICE PARTNERSHIPS—THREE PHASES OF THE POLICY

Phase One: 2005–2011

The first phase of local ICE partnerships began before school year (SY) 2005–2006 when Los Angeles County, California, and ICE formally inked the initial local 287(g) accord. Three additional counties (i.e., San Bernardino, California; Mecklenburg, North Carolina; and Riverside, California) adopted ICE partnerships after the beginning of SY 2005–2006 and before SY 2006–2007. These counties initiated the substantial uptick in agreements that occurred in the subsequent two years. After the beginning of SY 2006–2007 and before the start of SY 2007–2008, eighteen additional counties in twelve states adopted ICE partnerships. After the beginning of SY 2007–2008 and before the start of SY 2008–2009, another twenty-seven counties in thirteen states entered ICE partnerships. This was the single largest increase in the number of local jurisidictions partnering with ICE during phase one. There was a slowdown in the adoption of new agreements as the Obama administration took over, and no new agreements were established after the beginning of SY 2008–2009 and before SY 2009–2010. Then, after the beginning of SY 2009–2010 and before the start of SY 2010–2011, another six counties in five states adopted an ICE partnership. In total, local law enforcement agencies in fifty-five counties adopted an ICE partnership during phase one. During this phase, counties could enter a jail enforcement and or a task force type of partnership with ICE. The jail enforcement model allowed deputized local officers in local jails to identify and process individuals with pending criminal charges or criminal backgrounds arrested by local law enforcement agencies. The task force model allowed for the policing of immigration status violations in a range of other daily policing activities.

Figure 5.1 plots the counties that adopted ICE partnerships during this first phase of the policy. The counties in gray were those that adopted ICE partnerships. Importantly, ICE partnerships with local jurisdictions occurred across twenty different states in the United States during this period. Geographically, while most counties adopting the policy were somewhat close to the US-Mexico border, there were agreements established in northern regions of the nation (e.g., counties in Ohio and New Jersey).

FIGURE 5.1   US counties where ICE partnerships were enacted during phase 1 (2005–2011)

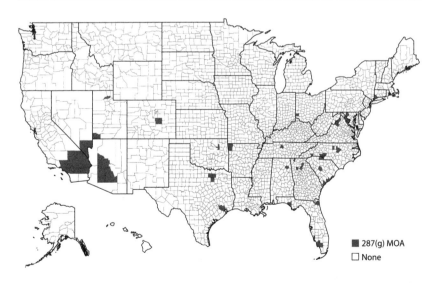

Notes: Gray-colored counties adopted 287(g) MOA during phase one (*N* = 55). Summary statistics illustrating key characteristics of these counties can be found in table 5.1.

To better understand the traits of these fifty-five counties, we explore a range of descriptive statistics about this sample in the year preceding the adoption of an ICE partnership, which are reported in table 5.1. On average, the cooperating counties had over two hundred schools, and about 45 percent of the schools were considered Title I–eligible schools. Being a Title I–eligible school indicates that the school had a relatively large share of students from low-income backgrounds.[11] The remaining rows of table 5.1 provide other educational, economic, and enforcement characteristics about these fifty-five counties one year before the start of the policy. The average share of Hispanic student enrollment in adopting counties was 22.1 percent. The Hispanic and non-Hispanic enrollment counts help illustrate that the counties in our sample tended to have large Hispanic student enrollment at all grade levels. Furthermore, we observe that non-Hispanic counts were also quite high and slightly larger than the Hispanic student counts. This indicates that populous counties were involved in ICE partnerships during phase one. Further, it suggests that in our adopting counties, Hispanic student enrollment was still smaller, on average, than non-Hispanic student enrollment.[12] In addition, we observe that about 41 percent of students in these counties were eligible for the National School Lunch Program and that the pupil-teacher ratio was just under seventeen. Furthermore, these counties issued relatively few immigration detainers in the year before treatment (i.e., 268 on average). Economically, these counties had unemployment rates that ranged between 2.2 and 11.1 percent and median household incomes just over $56,000.

Phase Two: 2012–2016

Phase two of the policy included a winding down of ICE partnerships nationwide and the emergence of other immigration enforcement programs. In 2012, the Obama administration announced a formal phasing out of ICE partnerships authorized under section 287(g). On December 31, 2012, all task force ICE partnerships were terminated. Jail enforcement ICE partnerships that existed at this time were allowed to continue, but new ICE partnerships were not sought in the subsequent years. By 2016, ICE partnerships with twenty-four counties remained. All were of the jail enforcement form and had been originally established before the phasing

TABLE 5.1   Baseline summary statistics for 287(g) MOA adopting counties in phase 1

VARIABLE	MEAN	STD. DEV.	MIN	MAX
Total Schools in County	209	334	4	1,980
Title I Schools in County	108	211	2	1,276
% Title I Schools in County	45.1	18.8	4.6	85.9
% Hispanic Enrollment	22.1	16.5	3.4	61.7
Hispanic Enrollment	58,103	159,429	505	1,069,267
Elementary School (K–5)	29,088	77,619	274	514,287
Middle School (6–8)	13,259	36,425	115	243,715
High School (9–12)	15,207	42,401	104	285,440
% Non–Hispanic Enrollment	70.5	17.6	27.1	95.7
Non–Hispanic Enrollment	76,220	91,433	1,200	469,771
Elementary School (K–5)	33,834	39,527	572	192,554
Middle School (6–8)	17,744	21,375	268	110,538
High School (9–12)	24,320	29,911	360	156,764
% NSLP–Eligible	41.1	12.6	12.7	65.7
Pupil–Teacher Ratio	16.5	2.7	13.4	23.7
Enacted 287(g) MOA at some point between 2005–11	1	0	1	1
Type of Enacted 287(g) MOA: Jail	0.84	0.37	0	1
Type of Enacted 287(g) MOA: Task Force	0.45	0.50	0	1
Type of Enacted 287(g) MOA: Jail & Task Force	0.29	0.46	0	1
Immigration Detainers Issued	268	748	0	4922
Unemployment Rate	5.3	1.8	2.2	11.1
Median Household Income	56,141	14,851	37,264	111,582

Notes: The summary statistics reported above are for the counties that ever adopted an ICE partnership between 2005 and 2011 ($N = 55$). The statistics reported are from the year prior to when the county first adopted an ICE partnership. The student enrollment and educational data are from the National Center for Education Statistics. The immigration enforcement data are from the ICE division of the Department of Homeland Security. The economic data are from the Local Area Unemployment Statistics published by the Bureau of Labor Statistics and the Small Area Income and Poverty Estimates reported by the U.S. Census Bureau.

out of the program. Importantly, a core component of the Obama administration's rationale for the phase-out of the agreements authorized by section
287(g) was the emergence of other programs allowing for partnering with
local agencies (i.e., Secure Communities, Priority Enforcement Program,
and E-Verify).

The Secure Communities program shared biometric information of
those individuals booked into local jails with ICE. When an individual's
information was shared, ICE officials were able to evaluate the case and
issue an immigration detainer until ICE could take custody of the individual. This more passive data-sharing program began rolling out in 2008
and was operational in all local jurisdictions nationwide by 2013. It was
discontinued in November 2014, during the Obama administration, but
was reinitiated in early 2017 by the Trump administration. The Priority
Enforcement Program took the place of Secure Communities between late
2014 and 2017. That program enabled ICE to take custody of individuals
who posed "a danger to public safety" and had a strong focus on convicted
criminals. It was more consistent with the "felons not families" policy of the
second term of the Obama administration.

Finally, the E-Verify program enabled cooperation from local jurisdictions. E-Verify allows employers to determine the employment eligibility of
potential employees by comparing an individual's Employment Eligibility
Verification form to records available through DHS and the Social Security Administration. Participation is technically voluntary; however, many
states have instituted requirements that large employers use E-Verify. In
2008, a total of 88,244 employers participated in the program. That number has steadily increased over time, and in 2017, the cumulative number
of employers participating reached 745,633.[13]

Taken together, these other programs involving local jurisdictions in immigration enforcement changed the intensity of immigration enforcement
felt nationwide. While ICE partnerships declined during phase two, other
more passive enforcement programs became more widespread.

Phase Three: 2017–present

Phase three is marked by a major expansion of ICE partnerships authorized
under section 287(g). This expansion began after the issuance of an execu-

tive order on January 25, 2017, directing ICE to seek the establishment of these partnerships "to the extent permitted by law."[14] This executive order was among the first issued after the Trump administration assumed power. It specified a federal policy that took a far more aggressive approach to the establishment of these accords with local law enforcement. This phase of agreements allowed for the development of jail enforcement agreements, an approach dating to the earlier phase of 287(g) agreements. It also introduced a new form of ICE partnership referred to as the Warrant Service Officer (WSO) agreement. Under WSO agreements, ICE provides more limited training to local officers, who then can execute ICE administrative warrants of arrest in local jails or correctional facilities. WSO agreements afford narrower enforcement authority to local officers, but also provide substantially less training to officers than the jail enforcement model. Task force agreements remain discontinued.

Between January 20, 2017, and the beginning of SY 2017–2018, a total of twenty-three new ICE partnerships were established. This marked the first set of new accords since SY 2011–2012 and nearly doubled the number of active agreements. After the start of SY 2017–2018 and before the beginning of SY 2018–2019, an additional fourteen new ICE partnerships were established. Then, after the start of SY 2018–2019 and before the beginning of SY 2019–2020, another twenty-one new ICE partnerships were signed. The largest increase in the number of partnerships, however, occurred after the start of SY 2019–2020 and before the beginning of SY 2020–2021. During this period, an additional fifty-two ICE partnerships were initiated with local law enforcement agencies across the nation. As of June 2020, there are 134 active ICE partnerships in jurisdictions across the United States.

Figure 5.2 plots the counties that adopted ICE partnerships during phase three. The counties in gray were those that had active ICE partnerships after SY 2016–2017 and before June 1, 2020. During phase three, ICE partnerships were occurring across twenty-three US states, more than participated during phase one. Additionally, we observe a greater concentration of agreements in a small number of states. In particular, counties in Texas and Florida account for 53 percent of all current ICE partnerships. Interestingly, the ICE partnerships in Florida are largely of the WSO model,

FIGURE 5.2   US counties where ICE partnerships were enacted during
phase 3 (2017–present)

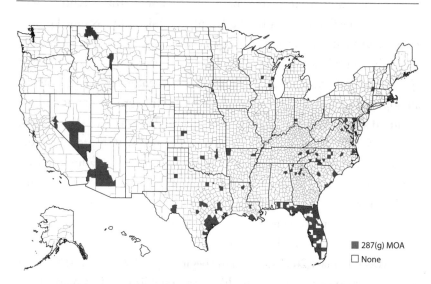

■ 287(g) MOA
□ None

Notes: Gray-colored counties adopted 287(g) MOA during phase three (*N* = 134). Summary statistics illustrating key characteristics of these counties can be found in table 5.2.

while the ICE partnerships in Texas were primarily enacted under the jail enforcement model. Geographically, most counties adopting the policy are somewhat close to the US-Mexico border, though yet again we observe substantial geographic diversity in adopting counties. For example, new partnerships have emerged in northern counties located in Montana, Wisconsin, and Massachusetts. Notably, there are no active ICE partnerships with counties in California or Utah during phase three.

Table 5.2 presents a set of descriptive statistics for the 134 adopting counties during phase three. On average, these counties had fewer public schools than adopting counties in phase one. Further, we observe that the percent of Title I–eligible schools in these counties was about 69 percent. This suggests that adopting counties enroll more low-income students during phase three (69 percent) than during phase one (45 percent). Furthermore, Hispanic student enrollment is substantially lower in the adopting counties during phase three. This suggests that ICE partnerships during phase three are less likely to be adopted by traditional immigrant destinations (e.g., counties

TABLE 5.2   Baseline summary statistics for 287(g) MOA adopting counties in phase 3

VARIABLE	MEAN	STD. DEV.	MIN	MAX
Total Schools in County	66	128	1	1,247
Title I Schools in County	44	81	1	734
% Title I Schools in County	68.9	20.0	20	100
% Hispanic Enrollment	22.9	18.1	0.2	71.6
Hispanic Enrollment	11,621	34,378	32	322,127
Elementary School (K–5)	5,608	16,336	0	151,962
Middle School (6–8)	2,683	7,974	0	74,502
High School (9–12)	3,326	10,060	0	95,536
% Non–Hispanic Enrollment	67.1	17.6	22.4	93.7
Non–Hispanic Enrollment	25,229	41,890	47	356,691
Elementary School (K–5)	11,367	18,854	20	158,298
Middle School (6–8)	5,868	9,848	13	85,127
High School (9–12)	7,986	13,215	14	113,084
% NSLP–Eligible	52.50	14.07	9.06	82.54
Pupil–Teacher Ratio	15.5	2.2	9.3	28.4
Active 287(g) MOA at some point after 2017	1	0	1	1
Type of Enacted 287(g) MOA: Jail	0.57	0.50	0	1
Type of Enacted 287(g) MOA: Warrant	0.45	0.50	0	1
Type of Enacted 287(g) MOA: Jail & Warrant	0.02	0.15	0	1
Immigration Detainers Issued	98	392	0	4,116
Unemployment Rate	4.4	1.0	2.6	9.2
Median Household Income	55,839	14,390	34,390	100,431

Notes: The summary statistics reported above are for the counties that ever had an active ICE partnership after 2017 (*N* = 134). The statistics reported are from the 2016–17 school year. The student enrollment and educational data are from the National Center for Education Statistics (NCES). The % NSLP-Eligible variable had some missingness in reporting for counties from Arizona, Florida, Massachusetts, Ohio, Nevada and Tennessee from the NCES data. We replace these missing values with values from other publicly available data. The immigration enforcement data are from the ICE division of the Department of Homeland Security. The economic data are from the Local Area Unemployment Statistics published by the Bureau of Labor Statistics and the Small Area Income and Poverty Estimates reported by the U.S. Census Bureau.

in California) and more likely to be adopted in more sparsely populated regions of the country.

We also observe that non-Hispanic student enrollment is more than twice as large as Hispanic student enrollment in these counties. The percent of students eligible for the National School Lunch Program is larger in the counties that adopted the policy in phase three. Further, we see a more even split between the types of ICE partnerships: about 57 percent were made as jail enforcement agreements and 45 percent were under the new WSO model. In 2 percent of counties, both types of agreement were operational. Immigration detainers issued in these counties before the adoption of the policy were lower on average than they were in phase one, but had a similar range. Further, while the unemployment rate was lower in adopting counties during phase three, we also observe that the nominal median household income was lower.

With all this information, it becomes clear that the typical county adopting the policy in phase three was smaller, had fewer schools overall, and had higher concentrations of poverty than the adopting counties in phase one. The Hispanic student population was also lower in these communities and was typically much smaller relative to the non-Hispanic student population. These communities, therefore, were less likely to be traditional immigrant destinations, but rather appear to be communities that experienced a sizable uptick in the immigrant population during the 2000s.

ICE PARTNERSHIPS, IMMIGRATION DETAINERS, AND STUDENT ENROLLMENT (PHASE ONE)

In this section, we present quasi-experimental evidence on the effect of ICE partnerships on the number of immigration detainers and on student enrollment during phase one. We focus on this phase of policy run-up because data are more fully available.

Immigration Detainers

To better understand the initial adoption of these policies, we explore the effect of ICE partnerships on the issuance of immigration detainers during phase one.[15] Immigration detainers authorize local law enforcement to continue holding an individual in custody for an additional two days (or more if those two days include weekends and holidays), so that ICE has time to review the case and potentially take custody of the individual. While ICE encourages local jurisdictions to honor these detainers, the decision to authorize the detainer is at the discretion of the local law enforcement agency. Using a sample of counties that applied to establish an ICE partnership with the DHS before 2012, we study the change in immigration detainers.

To do this, we link twelve years of county-year data for this subset of counties. In particular, we merge economic data, educational data, and immigration enforcement data over time and apply a difference-in-differences (DD) identification strategy.[16] This widely used quasi-experimental research design leverages the simultaneous availability of both cross-sectional data (i.e., from both adopting and nonadopting counties) and time-series data (i.e., data from both before and after the policy was put into place in a given county). The intuition of the DD design is straightforward. The first difference is effectively the change in a given outcome in a "treated" county before and after the policy adoption. This change reflects both the impact of the partnerships and the effects of time-varying determinants. The corresponding change in "control" counties provides a measure of these other time-varying determinants that can be used to isolate the impact of the policy (i.e., by calculating the difference in the two differences). This approach is implemented in advanced statistical analyses that control for the time-invariant characteristics of the counties in our sample (i.e., through county fixed effects) and common shocks that were unique to each given year and that affect all counties in the sample (i.e., through year fixed effects). This empirical approach aligns with the methodology used in our prior research with one substantive difference: we now include data about the share of schools in the county that qualified for Title I–eligible status. This allows us to consider results overall and for counties with high concentrations of poverty. This is critically important because, schools in these communities tend to face significant challenges with limited resources.

To compute a proxy for the intensity of poverty within a county, we divide the total number of schools in that county by the number of Title I–eligible schools. To avoid concerns about the potential endogeneity of this result, we rely on the intensity of poverty measured in the school year before the adoption of the ICE partnership. Counties where more than 40 percent of the county's schools were Title I–eligible schools were flagged as counties with high concentrations of poverty. We then restrict our sample to counties that both applied to establish ICE partnerships and met this high-poverty definition. Doing this means that we retain about two-thirds of the sample used in prior work.

For immigration detainers, we consider our results overall (reported as the gray dashed line in figure 5.3) and then compare these results to those for the sample of applying counties with high concentrations of poverty (reported as the black solid line in the figure). The figure 5.3 depicts point estimates from the event study DD specification that shows the emergence of an effect in the year leading up to the first school year when the policy

FIGURE 5.3   The effects of ICE partnerships on immigration detainers over time, by sample (phase one)

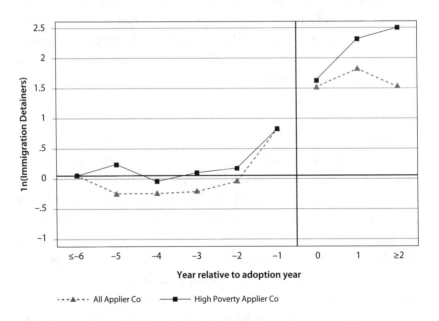

Notes: The black square plotted point estimates represent the sample of applier counties with high concentrations of poverty (*N* = 1,232). The gray triangle plotted point estimates represent the full sample of applier counties (*N* = 1,862). The model presented is an event study DD specification. The black vertical line denotes the beginning of treatment. Point estimates prior to adoption are not statistically significant. Each point estimate after adoption is statistically significant at ($p < 0.05$).

was in place and in the years immediately following policy adoption.[17] The effects in the adoption year and the subsequent years are statistically significant ($p < 0.05$). The effects before the adoption year are not statistically significant.

These results demonstrate two important details. First, they clearly show that ICE partnerships had a substantial effect on immigration detainers overall. Immigration detainers increase dramatically following the adoption of ICE partnerships. Second, the effect of ICE partnerships on immigration detainers was larger and grew more rapidly over time for counties with high concentrations of poverty. This pattern is consistent with at least two broad hypotheses, neither of which is mutually exclusive. One is that the enforcement activity done under the aegis of ICE-police partnerships may be more aggressive in higher-poverty communities. Second, there may also be a larger concentration of undocumented residents in higher-poverty communities.[18]

Student Enrollment

Our prior research examines the relationship between student enrollment in K–12 education and ICE partnerships that were enacted between 2005–2011.[19] Using the sample of counties that applied to establish an ICE partnership with the DHS, that study finds that the adoption of an ICE partnership led to a decline in Hispanic student enrollment by approximately 10 percent within two years. No effect from the policy was identified for non-Hispanic students. This result is powerful not only because it suggests that ICE partnerships had strong and consequential educational effects, but also because it implies a large demographic effect of the policy. Prior research studying the demographic effect of these policies has reported mixed effects across studies that largely relied on self-reported data.[20] Most suggest a null effect or a slightly negative effect. However, these results may be biased if survey data were misreported, which may explain some of the inconsistency.

Importantly, prior research has not yet explored if there were heterogenous effects of the policy for counties with higher concentrations of poverty during phase one. A massive body of literature indicates that poverty is an important factor influencing educational outcomes.[21] In this chapter, we examine the effect of ICE partnerships on student enrollment in counties with high concentrations of poverty.

Figure 5.4 presents the main results of ICE partnerships during phase one for both the high-poverty sample constructed here and the original sample using the full set of applying counties. Our main result can be seen in the first bar to the left, which depicts a statistically significant negative result of more than 11 percent. This result indicates that the effect of adopting an ICE partnership was a decline in Hispanic student enrollment by approximately 11 percent. The second bar presents the results for the full sample as reported in our prior research.[22] In the full sample of applier counties, we see a large and statistically significant decline in Hispanic student enrollment by more than 7 percent following adoption of an ICE partnership. However, the effect is smaller in magnitude than the estimated effect for high-poverty counties. The third and fourth columns presented in the figure demonstrate that the adoption of an ICE partnership had no effect on non-Hispanic student

FIGURE 5.4 The effects of ICE partnerships on student enrollment, by ethnicity and samples (phase one)

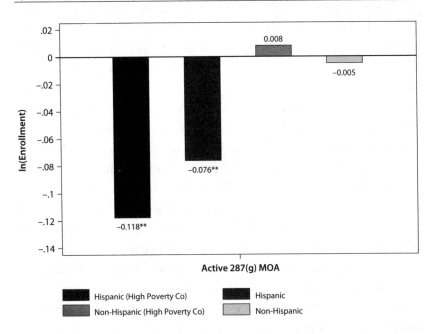

Notes: The results from columns (1) and (3) rely on a sample of applier counties with high concentrations of poverty ($N = 1,232$). The results from columns (2) and (4) rely on the full sample of applier counties ($N = 1,862$).

enrollment in high-poverty counties or the full sample of counties applying for these partnerships. These results indicate that the policy had more severe negative effects in high-poverty counties during phase one.

In addition to these main results from the "static" DD approach (i.e., where we assume a constant treatment effect over time), we also explore the "semi-dynamic" effects of ICE partnerships during phase one. In this semi-dynamic DD approach, we allow for treatment effects to vary based on the amount of time elapsed since the initiation of an ICE partnership. This provides the ability to discern if the magnitude of effects changes over time. In particular, we explore the effects on Hispanic and non-Hispanic enrollment by poverty status in the adoption year, one year later, or two or more years later. Figure 5.5 depicts these results.

FIGURE 5.5   The dynamic effects of ICE partnerships on student enrollment, by ethnicity and samples (phase one)

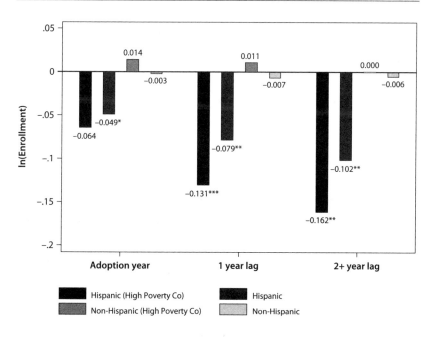

Notes: The results from bars (1), (3), (5), (7), (9), and (11) rely on a sample of applier counties with high concentrations of poverty (*N* = 1,232). The results from bars (2), (4), (6), (8), (10), and (12) rely on the full sample of applier counties (*N* = 1,862). Point estimates are reported above each bar.

We observe that effects in high-poverty counties are consistently more negative for Hispanic student enrollment than in the full sample. Furthermore, we observe that effects grow larger over time for those counties. In the adoption year, we see a decline by about 6 percent, which is not statistically significant. After one year of policy implementation, we see evidence that Hispanic student enrollment dropped by more than 13 percent. After two or more years of an active agreement, we observe that Hispanic student enrollment dropped by more than 16 percent. These latter two results are statistically significant at the ($p < 0.05$) level. These results are illustrated by the black bars. In all cases, the magnitude of the point estimate for the effects of ICE partnerships on Hispanic student enrollment over time were more negative for counties with high concentrations of poverty. We also find that the effect of the policy in high-poverty counties had no statistically significant impact on non-Hispanic student enrollment at any time after policy adoption as shown by the gray bars. The light-gray bars illustrate that this is also the case in the full sample of applier counties.

The findings presented here suggest that the effect of ICE partnerships was more severely felt in counties with high concentrations of poverty. This may be the case because enforcement efforts in these counties were more aggressive. In addition, undocumented residents tended to be more economically vulnerable during this time.[23] Therefore, the share of individuals most directly influenced by these policies was greater in counties with high concentrations of poverty. Given that adopting counties in phase three tended to have higher concentrations of poverty, the displacement effects observed in phase one may be further exacerbated during phase three. In sum, we find that the most vulnerable communities are likely the most negatively affected by these enforcement agreements.

GUIDANCE FOR COUNTIES CONSIDERING PROGRAM PARTICIPATION AND PRACTITIONERS

In no uncertain terms, our results from the implementation of ICE partnerships during phase one of the policy indicate large and ongoing student-displacement effects of adopting ICE partnerships, especially for counties with high concentrations of poverty. These effects likely harm educational outcomes in adopting counties in one or more of the following ways. For example, the reactive moves of Hispanic students triggered by the policy likely result in decreases to student achievement for this population. Empirical studies have documented the harmful developmental effects of such reactive moves, particularly for Hispanic and Black students and students who move frequently.[24] The psychological trauma induced by these policies may occur not only for students who move reactively but also for students who remain and live in a climate of aggressive local immigration enforcement.[25] These effects would also be magnified substantially if the policy induced students to drop out, which other evidence presented in this book suggests can be the case. The catastrophic and long-run economic consequences of dropping out of school are well documented.[26] Finally, the novel findings presented in this chapter suggest that the adoption of these policies in counties with high concentrations of poverty could be even more damaging, as their effects are larger in communities with more economic vulnerability. This heterogeneity is uniquely salient now. Our evaluation of the current phase three of these policies indicates that of the 134 counties that currently have active ICE partnerships, 125 meet our definition for being counties with a high concentration of poverty.

Our findings pertaining to the educational costs of such program participation should be a major consideration deterring interested counties from establishing ICE partnerships. The harmful social costs of this policy, however, are not limited to the K–12 educational sphere. Recent research finds that ICE partnerships also have deleterious effects on public health, housing, agricultural output, and other key economic indicators.[27] Of course, most of these conditions also affect the well-being of students and their ability to engage productively in school. The extant literature also indicates that these policies have no effect on the abatement of crime in adopting jurisdictions.[28] Furthermore, these partnerships may cause substantial harm to community policing endeavors due to the erosion of trust in local law enforcement.[29] The decline in the presence of Hispanic students is also likely to have pejorative, longer-term social consequences in communities that partner with ICE by reducing the scope for intergroup contact. An extensive literature in psychology finds that such intergroup contact is highly effective in reducing prejudicial attitudes and implicit biases.[30]

Taken together, this body of evidence clearly illustrates the harmful nature of these partnerships to adopting jurisdictions. The substantial educational, economic, and health consequences of these policies should be properly understood by jurisdictions entertaining the establishment or continuation of an ICE partnership. Given these realities, it is hard to see how a county would make a compelling evidence-based claim that the policy benefits outweigh the costs of establishing an ICE partnership. This is especially true given the evidence that the harmful educational effects grow larger over time.

However, practitioners may face a reality where an ICE partnership has been established in their jurisdiction as well as where they serve the students displaced by these policies. In these instances, we recommend that practitioners consider ways to prepare for the increased psychological trauma likely caused by these partnerships. In particular, prior literature suggests the value of providing culturally sensitive psychological support services for students, promoting healthy school environments that help increase understanding of cultural diversity, and maintaining healthy and safe classroom cultures and school climates.[31] Furthermore, mental health practitioners can play a key role in highlighting the increased need for psychological services.[32] Such approaches can also help combat discrimination related to perceptions of immigration status, which has been highlighted as a significant barrier to school involvement and success for some Hispanic students.[33]

CHAPTER 6

Educators are Stressed, Overworked, and Not Sure Whom to Trust

Legacy of the Trump Era

SHENA A. SANCHEZ, RACHEL E. FREEMAN, AND PATRICIA MARTÍN

E XACERBATING A HUNDRED YEARS of history of deporting immigrant communities, as discussed in chapter 1, deportations in the United States
were ramped up in the aftermath of 9/11 in 2001. While the Obama administration focused on deporting immigrants with a criminal record, the
Trump administration threatened to deport all undocumented immigrants
regardless of criminal background. Trump also harmfully targeted immigrant communities through his racist rhetoric and attempts to end federal
programs that protect immigrant communities. Even the COVID-19 pandemic did not slow the force with which the Trump administration exe-
cuted its draconian immigration policies.[1] In light of these realities, studies
show how immigrant students and their families resisted these forms of
oppression and faced tremendous fear and instability, which consequently
impacted their education.[2] Our study extends this discourse to include
public school educators, especially those who work closely with immigrant
students and their families.[3] We investigate how public school educators
were affected by and resisted the Trump administration's intensification of

immigration enforcement in order to understand the effects of these negative consequences on the entire school community.

We recruited respondents from a national survey of educators, "U.S. Immigration Enforcement Policy and its Impact on Teaching and Learning in the Nation's Schools," conducted by the Civil Rights Project in fall 2017 and 2018.[4] This larger study aimed to understand how immigration policy shifts in the first years of Trump's administration shaped American public education. Of the 3,600 respondents from the larger study, we invited a broad and representative sample of 159 educators, based on their role and the region in which they worked, to fill out an online questionnaire or participate in a phone interview. Of the 159 invited educators, 37 elected to participate in our study (27 respondents chose to complete the online questionnaire and 10 opted to do a phone interview) in the spring of 2018, one year after Trump's inauguration. Educators reported from thirteen states across the country, with the majority living in California and Tennessee. (See table 6.1 at the end of the chapter for details.)

We asked the same twelve items on the online questionnaire and in the phone interview, which focused on factors such as stress and anxiety levels, job satisfaction, working conditions, recruitment of new educators to the field, resource allocations, and recommendations for policy makers. A majority of the educators who expressed interest in participating in this study reported that they chose to respond because of their proximity to students who were affected by the harsh immigration policies and enforcement. One high school teacher from Tennessee stated, "Because I teach English as a second language, I work completely with immigrant students and I hear what they're thinking and saying and feeling and experiencing, so it was important to me to take part in this."

Our respondents explained that their schools served a large or increasing population of first- and second-generation immigrant students and families, and therefore, this topic put them "in the throes" of these issues, as one teacher put it. With this in mind, we note that the proximity of our respondents to large populations of students from immigrant backgrounds positions them to have a particularly important grasp of how immigration enforcement is impacting these students and their school communities. Additionally, some of the educators who elected to participate in this study report that they did

TABLE 6.1   Phone and online questionnaire interview logs

TYPE OF POSITION	STATE/REGION*	TYPE OF SCHOOL	POSITION DETAILS	INTERVIEW TYPE
Administrator	California	Elementary		Online
Administrator	Midwest	District level		Online
Administrator	Maryland	Elementary		Online
Administrator	Midwest	District level		Online
Administrator	New Jersey	PreK–8		Online
Administrator	Oregon	Elementary		Online
Administrator	Tennessee	Elementary		Online
Teacher	Arizona	Middle School	English Language Development teacher and co-coordinator of English Language Development program	Phone
Teacher	California	Elementary	Kindergarten teacher	Phone
Teacher	Florida	High School	ESOL teacher	Phone
Teacher	Georgia	Elementary	ESOL teacher	Phone
Teacher	Oregon	High School	Works for a support program for frequent absences	Phone
Teacher	Tennessee	Elementary		Phone
Teacher	Tennessee	High School		Phone
Teacher	Tennessee	High School		Phone
Teacher	Arizona	High School		Online
Teacher	Arizona	High School		Online
Teacher	California	Elementary School		Online
Teacher	California	High School		Online
Teacher	California	High School		Online
Teacher	Georgia	Middle School		Online
Teacher	Maryland	High School		Online

(continues)

TABLE 6.1 *Continued*

TYPE OF POSITION	STATE/REGION*	TYPE OF SCHOOL	POSITION DETAILS	INTERVIEW TYPE
Teacher	Massachusetts	Middle School		Online
Teacher	Nebraska	High School		Online
Teacher	New Jersey	Elementary and Middle		Online
Teacher	Oregon	High School		Online
Teacher	Tennessee	Elementary School		Online
Teacher	Tennessee	Elementary School		Online
Teacher	Tennessee	Elementary School		Online
Teacher	Tennessee	Middle School		Online
Teacher	Tennessee	High School		Online
Teacher	Tennessee	High School		Online
Teacher	Texas	Middle School		Online
Other certified	Arizona	K–12		Online
Other certified	California	High School	Counselor	Online
Other certified	California	High School	School psychologist	Online
Other certified	Oregon	High School	Comprehensive counselor	Phone
Other certified	Oregon	High School	Clinical mental health counselor intern	Phone

*Note: State names for interviewees at the district level are not disclosed to protect respondent confidentiality.

so because they care deeply about their students and want to inform others of the unanticipated consequences of immigration policies that exacerbated many of the challenges already plaguing public schools.

Two-thirds of the educators in our sample work in Title I schools, further adding to the complexities and stress of serving students from low-income and historically disadvantaged backgrounds. Some educators worry about their students being vulnerable to immigration enforcement in addition to lacking adequate resources and living in poverty. Our study reveals that educators who are adversely affected by the intensification of immigration enforcement can experience the following: (1) an increase in their levels of stress and anxiety; (2) an increase in their workload and shift in their professional responsibilities; (3) a deterioration in the sense of trust and community among their colleagues.

EDUCATORS ARE ANXIOUS AND STRESSED

This section discusses findings on the effects of intensified immigration enforcement on educators' well-being, with a particular focus on stress and anxiety. Respondents in our study report experiencing what they often refer to as "secondhand trauma," which we define as experiences related to feelings of emotional pain and despair as a result of caring for and about children who are undergoing distressing circumstances. These can include students' accounts of the harm experienced by their families, their fears of immigration raids taking place in their community, and their anxiety about immigration agents detaining their loved ones. We do not use trauma to denote a clinical assessment, but rather to echo the ways in which educators describe their students' experiences with heightened immigration enforcement.

Although we were not aiming to clinically label trauma, it is noteworthy that the effects of these stressful experiences on teacher well-being are consistent with the symptoms of secondary traumatic stress (STS), which is "the emotional duress that results when an individual hears about the firsthand trauma experiences of another."[5] Educators in our study report experiencing some symptoms of STS, including an acute increase in their levels of stress, anxiety, and worry due to the precarity of the immigration status of their students and students' families. Although STS has not been empirically studied among educators, especially for those who serve students experiencing traumatic events, there has been some research done on STS as experienced by social workers. Research on STS among social workers suggests that the emotional and psychological risks associated with caring about and serving vulnerable populations may be "an underestimated occupational hazard for those providing social work services."[6] To this end, our study suggests that some of the impacts on educator well-being and their symptoms that align with STS may be observed in the same way that prior research has recognized with social workers.

Consistent with symptoms of STS, educators report feeling a sense of helplessness with regard to how they can care for and support their students from immigrant backgrounds. Julie, an elementary school administrator from Tennessee, said, "This past year, my job has felt simultaneously more important and more pointless than it ever has before. Pointless because I feel helpless. I feel like math and science pale in comparison to safety, security, and family stability. But how do I affect that? How do I truly help my students? More important because I know that we are a safe place for our students and now, more than ever, that's what our children need."

Similar to Julie, Taylor, a high school teacher in Maryland, said of the impact of Trump's policies: "I approach my job with less hope." Many educators like Julie and Taylor expressed this sense of helplessness when it comes to being able to support their students and their families.

Educators also report an increase in their students' stress levels from the fear of a lack of safety in school, in their community, and at home. Joel, a high school teacher in Oregon, said, "It impacts me to see the mixture of dread and resignation that I sense from my students and their families." Similarly, Amanda, an elementary school teacher in New Jersey, said, "It breaks my heart to see nine-year-olds worry about their safety and the security of their families." Katherine, another high school teacher from Oregon, summed up what other educators in our study noted about student stress, "It's fear of something happening in general while they are at school and they come home and everything has changed. There's a lot of stress around this."

There is a consistent pattern of educators feeling unsure about how to help their students cope with the fear of going home and finding that a family member has been detained or deported. An elementary school teacher from Tennessee, Deborah speaks to the bond she has with her students, particularly her Latina/o and ELL students, which is also echoed by other educators in our study. Speaking empathetically about her students, Deborah said:

> I know that they are going through a little bit more with immigration; they have to worry about coming home and having that fear of walking home and "oh, is my mom going to be here? Is my dad going to be here? Is my

sister or my auntie going to be here?" along with all the other stresses of coming from a low-income area as well.

As a result of this closeness with their students, a majority of the educators in our study report experiencing "heightened stress," as one teacher put it, which affects their ability to teach in a climate of intensified immigration enforcement. Rebecca, a teacher from Oregon, describes her stress and its impact on her work:

> There's been a great deal of stress. Partly in just—how do I talk to my kids and what's going on and what do I say and not say and just as I hear things, it's like "okay, how is it going to affect me in my work? What do I need to think about? What do I need to do?" I have noticed increased anxiety as new things [policies] are released and new things [rhetoric] are said and done.

Most educators enter the teaching profession because they enjoy working with children and developing meaningful relationships with their students as well as believe in an ethic of care.[7] However, what is often left unaddressed are the ways that these qualities make teachers more vulnerable to experiencing higher levels of stress and anxiety when they witness their students going through traumatic events.

Consequently, this increase in stress significantly impacts the emotional and physical well-being of our respondents. Julie reports losing sleep, worrying about how her school will care for students should their parents be deported. She discussed feeling emotionally fatigued as she thinks through the option of taking students into her personal care:

> Working at a low-income, high-priority, high-risk school always comes with a certain amount of added stress. This past year, that anxiety and stress increased drastically. How do I tell a sobbing child that it's going to be okay, that their parents are waiting for them—safe and sound at home—when I know there's a strong possibility that's not true? I have found myself lying awake at night agonizing over whether I should offer to take temporary custody of a child or children in the event that their parents are deported unexpectedly, and that's emotionally exhausting in an entirely new way.

Angela, an elementary school administrator in Oregon, echoed Julie's sentiments, sharing, "Some days it's hard to get up and face everything under this administration." Angela's and Julie's experiences are not unusual among educators in our study. We find that our respondents feel a deep sense of responsibility to their students beyond their classrooms and the schoolhouse doors. In a climate of heightened immigration enforcement, it is imperative to understand the ways in which the well-being of teachers and administrators has been impacted as they care for their students.

EDUCATORS ARE OVERWORKED

Along with heightened anxiety and stress, we find that the intensification of immigration enforcement also adversely impacted working conditions for educators. We define working conditions as the context in which educators carry out their roles, including workload, time demands, and responsibilities. A majority of the educators in our study work in Title I schools and faced multiple challenges even before Trump coming into office. Jessica, an elementary school teacher in California said,

> We are facing a slashing of our budget . . . which means we are going to lose some personnel, we are going to lose intervention programs, we are going to lose a lot of stuff . . . [T]here is nothing I can do about that. We need more money. So does every other school right, especially the Title I schools. Now we have to decide what we are going to cut.

Compounding the obstacles that have existed in underresourced schools for decades, the Trump administration's escalation of immigration enforcement put further stress on educators' workload. For example, Tanya, an elementary school ESL teacher from Georgia, described how the recent intensification substantially added to her workload as she took on additional responsibilities to care for her students and their parents:

> I feel like this year . . . I have been working harder because I want my kids to know how much I love them . . . so I feel like it is a heightened of doing extra and going above and beyond because I find myself during some of

the breaks and stuff like "I am very tired," you know? And stuff needs to get done because you are trying to do extra and supplement and giving the parents what they need . . . I have been doing it [extra work] when a parent needs, you know, the conferences or a question or needs things, so just doing extra because like I said, I don't know if I will see them tomorrow, so I want to make sure that the last time that I did interact with this person has been the best interaction possible. So I feel like it [the stress] is just heightened, you know? So it is just . . . stressful, you know? I try to tell myself not to be stressed out, but it's just not knowing what tomorrow brings that's kind of . . . it's not a nice feeling.

These expansions in professional responsibilities mean that educators, especially those who are already working overtime to care for their underserved students, are even more strained and at a greater risk for burnout and experiencing secondhand trauma.[8]

Additionally, educators in our study report spending more time to address the needs of students and families impacted by immigration policies, causing them to take time away from classroom instruction. Our respondents make a concerted effort to keep up with immigration policies so that they may provide accurate information to their students—this too takes a significant amount of time in addition to their teaching responsibilities. Alex, a middle school teacher from Arizona, described:

And the other thing is trying to get information for myself as a teacher about how I can support students who are being negatively impacted by that [immigration enforcement]. The University . . . has some organizations within [that] are trying to disseminate that kind of information, so I'm just trying to be aware of what's going on myself, so that I can share that information with my students and their families.

Like Alex, other educators in our study feel that they often have to independently educate themselves about changes in immigration legislation to best serve their students. Clarissa, a middle school teacher in Massachusetts, said, "I have been constantly checking the news, district immigration info website, and other resources for updates and information about the constantly changing policies of the administration." The additional time it takes to do this, along with the need to ensure they are getting current and accurate information, becomes overwhelming and contributes to the increase in their levels of anxiety and stress. Furthermore, while many teachers strive to inform their students on immigration matters, they are concerned that it also takes away from students' time to learn academic content. Katie, a high school teacher from Tennessee, described this dilemma:

> I have had to have conversations with my students about how important it is to follow the rules—driving the speed limit, wearing seat belts, not being rowdy in public because it might attract attention. I feel like this is beyond my responsibilities as a teacher, and the frequent need to discuss immigration policy detracts from actual education time.

Our findings support extant research on the negative impacts that the added burdens of obtaining information about immigration enforcement policies and ways to better support their students has on instructional time and, consequently, teaching efficacy.[9] Teachers in this study feel that their new responsibilities call them to take on many additional roles (e.g., social worker, counselor, and legal advocate) since their school does not provide these experts. Alex, a teacher from Arizona, commented, "I think that if the state . . . had more supports for students and their families, I could be more of a teacher, I guess more percentage of the time and less like a . . . legal advocate and stuff like that."

Similarly, it became increasingly difficult for educators to keep fearful immigrant students engaged in their schoolwork under the Trump administration, and teachers found themselves frequently comforting students. Tanya shared her experience reassuring students who are fearful of immigration enforcement, stating, "That has made my job hard because you never know when you've got to stop and be a counselor to a child and letting them know they are safe, they are secure."

Across the board, we find that educators regularly grapple with the best ways to provide their immigrant students and families with support and comfort in a time of intensified immigration enforcement while maintaining the quality and rigor of their instruction. In short, we find that educators' sense of urgency and helplessness, in addition to stress and anxiety, place additional burdens on their already heavy workloads.

DETERIORATING TRUST AMONG EDUCATORS
AND ACROSS THE SCHOOL COMMUNITY

As respondents in this study reported shifts in their workload, time distribution, and responsibilities, they also expressed mounting distrust within their school community. Trust within a school's community is a critical factor in creating an environment where all of its members—students, educators, and parents—can thrive. For immigrant students and their families who are vulnerable to detention and deportation, trust in schools is especially important, as they may hesitate to share personal information about their status with educators or participate in school activities that they perceive could put them at risk.[10] Considering that the immigrants targeted by Trump's deportation policies often send their children to under-resourced schools, there is an added layer of difficulty for educators to build trust with their students' families. Additionally, it is often challenging to foster a sense of trust in under-resourced schools because of factors such as a high teacher turnover, a disproportionate number of inexperienced teachers, and the underrepresentation of teachers of color.[11]

The intensified immigration enforcement has also led to a deteriorating sense of trust among educators, creating deeper fissures within the school community. Some of our respondents expressed uncertainty about whom they are able to trust to care for their immigrant students. Brenda, a district administrator in the Midwest, said, "I do not always know who I can trust—just like our students and families." Similarly, Audrey, a high school teacher in California, shared that she operates with caution when speaking with her colleagues and students because she does not trust them with sensitive matters, saying, "I am even more careful about what I say to students and what I say to other adults. I have lost trust in some of my colleagues and have a network of 'trusted' colleagues that I go to with these issues." Similar to Audrey, some educators are wary that their colleagues will not protect their students and, instead, will share private information about their students and their students' families if ICE agents came to their school. For example,

Caroline, an elementary school teacher in Tennessee, has taken steps to be more diligent about keeping her students' information safe, saying, "I make sure now to keep my students' records more carefully locked up." These concerns are shared by educators who work in districts that have officially declared noncooperation with ICE as well as districts that have not made official statements.

We find that even when a school district publicly states support for its immigrant students, educators in schools still worry their colleagues will not abide by the district's policies. Audrey, the teacher from California, said, "Our district policy is protective; unfortunately, some staff disagree and I fear they may act to report students to ICE." Elizabeth, who works for a school district in Tennessee that has not issued public statements opposing cooperation with ICE, feared that some school staff will release information to immigration agents because they have not received enough training about what to do if these officials came to their school. She described this concern and a desire for training around privacy to ensure that educators are not sharing information that will put their students and families at risk:

> I think that front office staff and front office volunteers, parent volunteers . . . all need to be retrained as far as access to student information because I think it would be really easy if someone walked up with a big shiny badge and acts very authoritatively for them to give out information that they're not supposed to because well it's the federal government, you know? It's ICE. So, we need specific training that the privacy rules still apply.

Educators in this study see themselves as protecting their students from federal agents, not collaborating with them to enforce Trump's immigration policies.

Along with a lack of trust in US government officials and a deterioration of trust among the educators themselves, our respondents also sensed that students' parents are afraid that schools will give ICE information about their immigration status. While strong parent-teacher relationships are critical to the academic success of students, research has shown that there often is a lack of trust between parents and educators in under-resourced schools that serve communities of color.[12] We find that the intensified immigration enforcement under the Trump administration exacerbated the challenges when building trust and a sense of community in schools, especially with parents. Educators reported that they have seen a decrease in parent volunteering in their schools and that parents have been reluctant to sign permission forms for their children to participate in activities such as field trips. Many teachers expressed that they are concerned about the decreasing parental engagement in schools because it is critical to the quality of their students' education. Teachers believe that the more parents are involved in school, the more engaged their students are in the classroom. Deborah, an elementary school teacher in Tennessee, summed up these observations:

> Parents have fallen back a little bit trying to keep a low radar, a low profile. They don't want to be seen too many places driving around especially I have noticed. A lot of them will walk and won't drive . . . because they are so worried that something might happen. So that kind of takes away the joy because I know that if the parents aren't involved then the students slack off more and have more behavioral issues and so parent involvement is important . . . if they're worried about their parents they are not going to be worried about how to do division.

To mitigate the negative effects that immigration enforcement has had on parents' trust in educators, some of our respondents have taken to spending more time reaching out to parents and families who have distanced themselves from the school community. For example, Daniela, a high school psychologist in California, said she focuses on "building rapport and letting families know that [she is] here to support and not report." Similarly, Katherine, a high school teacher in Oregon, described how the mounting distrust of families has influenced her communication approach: "Because there's a lot of fear of basically coming out about your visa status or your legal status . . . they live in that fear. And so it's affected me a lot at work and just how I communicate with the families." Like Katherine, other educators in our study seek to better understand the real risks and dangers their students' parents face while continuing to build parents' trust in their work so that they can better serve their students in spite of the hostile immigration environment.

EDUCATORS ARE MORE COMMITTED

In addition to our three major findings, we find that another consistent theme in our study is an increased commitment that educators have to their students from immigrant backgrounds. Despite the adverse effects on their well-being, increased workload, and growing distrust that they are experiencing, our respondents reported that they are continuing to work hard to protect and educate their immigrant students. Moreover, some of these educators feel a stronger sense of dedication to ensuring the safety and success of their vulnerable students. For example, Sasha, a high school teacher in Nebraska, said, "I can retire very soon, but I am *not*. I want to keep fighting!" Similarly, Jessica, an elementary school teacher in California, said, "I feel even more strongly about what I do." However, although educators we surveyed and interviewed expressed a deep commitment to teaching immigrant students, we cannot know to what extent this is true for all, or even most educators in these circumstances. We are concerned that the additional stress, overwork, and worries about trust in their working environment can lead to burnout and eventually the decision to leave their positions, exacerbating the already deep inequities in these schools. Research suggests that this is a real possibility.[13]

CONCLUSION AND RECOMMENDATIONS

Our study reveals that the intensified immigration enforcement has adversely affected the well-being of educators and school communities across the country in three major ways. First, educators are experiencing symptoms consistent with STS, specifically an increase in levels of anxiety and stress. Second, educators are overworked and burdened with responsibilities outside the scope of their profession, which makes it challenging for them to carry out their instructional objectives. Third, there is a deterioration of trust among school community members—parents have become increasingly concerned about whether schools are safe places for their children and educators fear that some of their colleagues will not protect their students. Elizabeth's experience as a high school Spanish teacher in Tennessee best captures these three findings, describing her experience when one of her students was detained by ICE:

> [My student] spent forty-nine days in custody and then he was finally re-leased because we were able to raise $8,500 . . . I was the one who got the 2 a.m. phone call from the jail because I made my kids memorize my cell phone number for emergencies . . . I was the only one who could commu-nicate between him and his dad for their safety. And so, spending forty-nine days trying to pass messages back and forth, trying to negotiate the legal system, trying to, you know, keep my kid calm. And then I had to tell my students at school, like, we have an empty desk . . . I told them with permis-sion from my student what happened and I broke down in front of them. And then I'm trying to hold them all together because I have an entire class of kids who know why their classmate isn't there and know it could happen to them, know it could happen to their families.

The educators in our study have numerous recommendations for pol-icy reforms and resources to improve their working conditions and overall well-being. First, educators suggest the urgent need for more staff (e.g., counselors, social workers, and interpreters) to support students from im-migrant backgrounds. They emphasize that having more educators available to care for students will strengthen school culture and make their commu-nity a safer and more welcoming environment for all. Katherine, a high school teacher in Oregon, explained, "The district does have some social workers, but they are spread pretty thin." Similarly, Daniela, a high school psychologist from California, said, "I would like my district to consider hiring social workers or case managers to support students."

Respondents also expressed the need for programs and adequate mental health care to help them navigate the secondhand trauma they experience. Angela, an elementary school administrator in Oregon, wrote:

> I'd like easier access to counseling myself. Even though I haven't been trau-matized yet, I'm constantly affected by students' experiences and fears, and

the abuses of ICE and this administration are constantly on my mind. I don't know how to move forward with my life with the constant shadow over me. I can't imagine how the kids and families cope.

States and local governments should consider building programs about navigating secondhand trauma related to being an educator. Additionally, we urge researchers in the field of psychology to conduct studies of educators' experiences associated with STS to improve the field's clinical understanding of educators' mental health and well-being. Educators in our study also want more professional development opportunities and workshops in immigration policies so that they may be better equipped to support their students. Katie, a high school teacher in Tennessee, expressed the need for information when educators are supporting their immigrant students: "It frustrates me how unsure I am about what would happen if one of my students was arrested for deportation. Am I allowed as a teacher to intercede? If the immigration policy goes into effect, I want to know step by step what will happen and what the school's response will be."

Beyond the school and district levels, our respondents expressed that the draconian approach to immigration enforcement—the raids, detentions, and deportations—is cruel and unwarranted. Audrey, a high school teacher in California, said: "The government needs to get out of the fear business. Coming to people's homes in the middle of the night, establishing checkpoints to pass through, and hassling all of us as we cross the border has not made our country safer, but it has made our country scarier."

Max, an elementary school teacher in California, said, "Stop splitting up families! Stop threatening groups of people based on religion and color of skin!" Max's sentiment is shared widely by other educators who also feel that policy makers are often uninformed about the lived experiences of their students. Respondents in this study called on leaders to understand that immigration raids could potentially be fatal for students. Elizabeth, a high school teacher in Tennessee, said, "The policies that are being put in place could result in my kids literally being sent back to their deaths. And I think policy makers need to look my kids in the face if they're going to make decisions like that." Educators are deeply concerned about their students' well-being and call on policy makers to discontinue threatening, policing, raiding, and breaking up immigrant communities.

We find that intensified immigration enforcement policies disrupt the school ecology and impact the well-being of entire school communities—educators, students, and families alike. While many educators remain committed to protecting their immigrant students in the face of what they perceive to be cruel terrorization, the stressful conditions under which they are forced to work are unsustainable and put them at risk for burnout.[14] Our findings suggest that educators are being pushed to their limits as they care deeply for their students and strive to support them.

CHAPTER 7

How Do Schools
Cope with Immigration
Enforcement?

PATRICIA GÁNDARA AND JONGYEON EE

A LL THAT WE HEARD from educators in our 2017–2018 national survey of educators left us with a deep desire to know how schools cope with the fear and chaos they routinely experience as a result of the terrorizing of immigrant communities by ICE. To answer this, we developed a set of framing questions that could help us understand the ways that districts respond to ICE threats. In this chapter, we present findings and lessons learned from interviews we conducted with administrators across the nation.

We explored the following topic areas in the interviews: the composition of the predominant immigrants living in that community, why or if ICE had targeted the community, and the general attitudes of the community or district regarding the immigrant student population; coping strategies at the school or district level for students from immigrant homes, their families, educators, and the broader community; types of support offered at the district level or higher (e.g., state department of education); and the unmet needs requiring additional resources and practices.

INTERVIEWS WITH ADMINISTRATORS

The Sample

All interviewees were either identified from our survey study of twenty-four districts (see chapter 2) or were recommended to us by various colleagues both in and outside of academe. We recruited administrators from each region of the country, guided by several considerations. First, we wanted a minimum of four individuals from each of the four census regions, including states with different political contexts. This resulted in four individuals from the Northeast and Midwest, and seven and six interviewees from the South and West, respectively. Second, given that different-sized districts would presumably have different administrative structures and different levels of resources, we also included districts of various sizes.[1] Third, we identified individuals from each district who had the greatest familiarity with district practices regarding immigrant students. This was usually a superintendent or assistant superintendent, but not always. In this regard, we found that sometimes the most knowledgeable person was actually the ELL teacher or coordinator at the district who functioned as an administrator with regard to immigrant issues. Finally, we deliberately selected educators with a proactive and supportive philosophy toward immigrant students, as we would be unlikely to learn much about a district's strategies from someone who did not support students from immigrant households and their families. Consequently, we recruited twenty-two interviewees, including ten superintendents or assistant superintendents, one state department of education director, one district administrator, one district board member, five principals or assistant principals, three teacher activists/organizers, and one consul general of Mexico (who was mentioned by administrators as an important resource). (See table 7.1.)

The Interviews

Interviews were semi-structured with a list of guiding questions and also allowed interviewees to pursue themes they or we considered important at the particular site. Interviews lasted for a minimum of forty-five minutes, were one-on-one (except one interview where the same school's principal and assistant principal jointly participated), and took place via Zoom or phone.

TABLE 7.1   Interview participants

REGION	STATE	NUMBER
Northeast	Massachusetts and New York	4
Midwest	Indiana, Missouri, Nebraska, and Ohio	4
South	Florida, Mississippi, Tennessee, and Texas	7
West	Arizona, California, Colorado, and Oregon	6
Other		1
Total		**22**

All interviews were recorded with the permission of interview participants and transcribed verbatim.

We talked to administrators in the spring of 2020, shortly after school closures had begun as a pandemic mitigation strategy. As a result, we heard a great deal about district strategies to deal with the pandemic and the grave concerns that administrators had about the very unequal impact the pandemic was having on immigrant students and their families. It was sometimes difficult to keep the focus on immigration enforcement as schools were so consumed with designing and delivering distance learning, particularly to low-resource students. The issue of the pandemic clearly unveiled a wide range of existing hardships experienced by immigrant students and their families, as they are the most marginalized population in many communities. Nonetheless, our goal was to understand the challenges associated with immigration enforcement policies, which will also presumably be with us after the pandemic and will continue to affect immigrant students and their schools.

Details of the Informants by Role

We categorized most of the twenty-two interview participants into three groups by their educational role: administrators from the state department of education, district superintendents, and principals or ELL coordinators. We next describe the three different categories, from the state department level to the classroom, and some of the informants' views and experiences shaped by their roles.

STATE DEPARTMENTS OF EDUCATION State departments of education do not generally set policy for how schools are to deal with immigration issues. The state legislature and the governor may establish statewide policies, like proclaiming the state a "sanctuary" state, but the department of education will simply follow suit and not contradict that policy. The job of the department is primarily to distribute funding and provide guidance and support for pedagogical issues and accountability. As such, when we inquired in many different states about the role that the state department of education played with respect to immigration enforcement affecting the schools, no one could come up with an example, with one exception. In this western state, department of education leaders were "pushing the envelope" to such an extent that we were told, "if we get a different governor, we may all be let go." They were pulling together community-based nonprofits across the state in regular meetings to make clear that the state's position was not to cooperate with ICE, and that they invited these groups to help support immigrant families and children. The department prepared "know your rights" materials for distribution to all schools and paid for the training and certification of notary publics so that immigrant parents could take care of official business at no cost in a place—the school—that felt safe and avoid becoming victims of unscrupulous individuals that prey on them.[2] The department was also "doing a lot of messaging" to the state superintendents' organization stressing antibullying against immigrants in the state. Perhaps most importantly, this activist department of education was setting a tone for the public schools that "immigrants are welcome here," which presumably filtered down to districts.

DISTRICT SUPERINTENDENTS OF SCHOOLS The real policy action in the public schools occurs at the district superintendent level. We interviewed ten superintendents or assistant superintendents in all regions of the country and in very large, medium, and small districts. The districts were also in urban and largely rural areas. In the cases where we spoke to assistant superintendents, it was because they had been handed the job of overseeing ELL and immigrant issues, which were often housed together in the same office. As we would not likely learn much from districts that were not actively trying to protect their immigrant students, or which had not experienced any enforcement issues, we initially focused on superintendents in districts that were known to have pro-immigrant student policies, whether these were formal or informal, or that had experienced the impact of enforcement directly. Some of the districts in our sample were in very conservative states and did not advertise their positions but were often as strong in defense of their immigrant students and families as those in sanctuary states. But this support could waiver with a change in superintendents.

Effective superintendents must navigate the politics, articulate a philosophy or district position, gather resources, and commit them. They must also implement the directives of their school board and maintain a working relationship with the board. In some cases, the board will have a well-articulated position, and this will guide the superintendent. In others, there will be little agreement among board members, and the superintendent is left to thread that needle. But in all cases, the superintendent does well to be highly cognizant of the various board members' stances. At least one superintendent was let go during the time of our study for failing to adhere to board policy with respect to immigrant students. If they are in a large district, they may delegate programmatic decisions to others, but the responsibility of staking out a position, defending it, and gathering the resources to allow the schools to respond to students' needs lay with the superintendent. States that have adopted a sanctuary position, like California, New York, and Illinois, make taking a position easy, though defending that position may not always be easy in all parts of the state. In states with strong anti-immigrant positions, such as Arizona, Georgia, or Oklahoma, navigating the politics can be challenging. And in states with very different regional attitudes, such as Texas and Florida, it's especially critical to have the support of the local school board. Of the ten superintendents that we interviewed, one was in a sanctuary state but in a very conservative rural area, one was in a largely conservative state but in a progressive area, and the rest were split between conservative and progressive (sanctuary) states.

PRINCIPALS AND ELL COORDINATORS   While the superintendent sets the tone and determines how resources to support the schools will be allotted (with the help of the school board), the principals must carry out the work, and their level of commitment to the community determines to a great extent the breadth and effectiveness of support for immigrant students and their families. In some districts, especially in "new destination" areas of the country (regions with relatively new immigration), the role of planning and coordinating services was handed over to the teacher who taught and coordinated the ELL program. These were the people who knew the students and families and in whom the students and families had the most trust. In our experience, these were also extraordinarily committed individuals with deep connections to community-based organizations (CBOs) that worked closely with the schools.

We interviewed individuals in all of these categories, plus a consul general with the Mexican government and a school board member/immigration activist, in five general areas of inquiry: (1) what shaped their philosophy or stance regarding immigration enforcement; (2) relationships with CBOs and other community partners; (3) strategies for supporting immigrant students and their families; (4) strategies for supporting teaching staff; (5) what they needed from policy makers.

LISTENING TO SCHOOL LEADERS

First, considering the interviews as a whole, what is most evident is that people in education, from state departments of education to the teacher in the classroom, see their jobs as educating all students in the community. Regardless of their particular political stance, educators educate, and it is difficult to find one who believes their job is anything other than to educate, to the best of their ability, all the students in their care. This is not to say that all educators are equally committed to all students, but even if for reasons of self-interest (e.g., appearing to be a successful teacher or keeping up student enrollment numbers in the school or district), overwhelmingly, educators are committed to serving the students that come their way. We heard this over and over. Even some educators who strongly opposed undocumented immigration conceded that their commitment to educating the children of immigrants took precedence over their political beliefs. While this may seem obvious, or perhaps even Pollyannaish, it is fundamental to understanding how the schools in deep-red states as well as in deep-blue states, and those in between, cope with the threat of immigration enforcement and its impact on students and their families. Educators are also acutely aware that students are attached to families, and if families are not functioning, then it makes educating students difficult. Of course, if students are not learning, schools and teachers appear to be ineffective, so some leave the schools that have many students whose families are unable to function adequately because of poverty, disorganization, and fear. But among those who choose to stay, there are amazing stories of dedication and humanity. Immigration enforcement activities tend to take place in very-low-income communities with immigrant families that are barely holding things together and in schools that are underresourced and overstressed. But our informants were clear that there is a role to play by each level of the education system, and especially its partners, in attempting to move students successfully to high school graduation and beyond.

Developing a Philosophy

In order to successfully confront the challenge of immigration enforcement as it affects the schools, school leaders have to come to terms with their own philosophy of educating immigrant students and become clear about their role in the process. We did not actually ask how individuals developed their philosophy about educating students in immigrant families, but many people wanted to talk about this, particularly those who had had encounters with ICE raids or deportations in their community. A superintendent in a conservative midwestern state recounted how he clarified his philosophy. About two weeks after a raid in his community that separated many children from their parents, and after the district worked diligently during that time to find places for them to stay if they lost their parents, he was called to a second-grade classroom by the principal. The teacher explained that the lesson for the day had dealt with heroes; the children were drawing their heroes on poster boards. One little girl had drawn a stick figure of a man and written, "This is Dr. X [the superintendent]. He keeps kids safe."

> I broke down when I saw that . . . But that's my driver. I can't walk in immigrant shoes. I can't. I'm a superintendent of schools. I'm educated. I grew up in a fairly middle-class family. But I can tell you that every day I go to work, I think about what my primary responsibility is. That's that little girl

and every child we have in our school system . . . [A]s I've seen the social wear and tear on families and kids over the years, I'm even more convinced that education is the one consistent in kids' lives that we have to make sure nothing happens to.

A school board member in a very red state reflected on her experience over several years with immigration enforcement in their schools and shared, "I just think now more than ever, we have to be really courageous, standing up and saying these children belong in our schools, that they deserve a world-class education and we have to do everything we can to help them." A Latina superintendent in a very conservative rural area in a progressive western state explained the "full service" schools she oversaw that provided for all kinds of social needs, food, housing, even funds to help bury family members, and how she did some of this with donations from individuals in the community who were not necessarily pro-immigrant. When asked how she was able to convince people to aid the immigrant families, she didn't tip her hand about personal beliefs. She simply asserted, "My philosophy is, let's remove the adults from the picture. Let's just do good things for kids . . . I just keep the focus on the kids. It's all about the kids." She went on to say, if these other superintendents knew the kids, "they'd maybe think differently." A state department of education director shared a similar thought, "We are here, the [X] Department of Education. We don't play politics, but our responsibility is to protect every single one of our children." This echoes the words of another superintendent in a conservative southern state, when asked what could be done to ease the burden on the students. Her response: "I would ask that they at least look at our children, and see what we can do to start from there."

Virtually all interviewees described their personal philosophies as a belief that grew with knowing the students and families, and from a sense of basic fairness that all students should have a stable education. And their job as educators was to somehow ensure that happened. One superintendent described the teachers as "the second mom or the second dad to a lot of those children." Evidently a similar sentiment sets in with members of these conservative communities when the immigrants put down roots. An ESL teacher from the South who coordinated the immigrant services for the district explained how many residents were shocked when raids occurred in their community. "They said, 'I didn't think that was what was meant by deportations. I didn't know they were going to deport this person or this person. I thought it was just criminals and things like that.'" As a result, there was an outpouring of support from nonimmigrant residents, donating and raising funds for the immigrants and their children. Evidently, these incidents with immigration enforcement have a clarifying effect on the beliefs and attitudes of many residents of these communities as well. As the teacher/administrator explained, "We also live in the Bible Belt; it's like, no, love your neighbor."

Partnerships with CBOs and Other National Nonprofits

When asked about the importance of partnering with CBOs to protect immigrant students, the school board member from the South replied in the same way almost all interviewees did: "It's absolutely essential." In describing their partner CBOs, we found that districts had an extraordinary web of services, some linked to national organizations, most able to mobilize rapidly, with deep connections to the communities in which these schools were located. All districts relied on them, whether in virulently anti-immigrant areas or in safe havens or sanctuary communities. A superintendent from a northeastern progressive state noted,

> I can't cross that line [to provide legal counsel], but the way we support our families is by supporting those community organizations . . . [F]amilies are often more comfortable with them than school district personnel. They have the safe spaces that the families were willing to come to when they were no longer willing to come to city buildings [the district building]. The district can offer a "know your rights" presentation, but more people will show up for the CBO.

Even in relatively well-funded districts like the one above, CBOs provide services that the schools cannot afford or cannot access. Legal clinics were mentioned a number of times, with ACLU and Catholic charities being named prominently. Mental health services and social workers were also provided in districts by local CBOs. A superintendent from the Midwest, who had dealt with ICE raids in his community, was very clear about the value of CBOs in his district: "We get lots of support and our liaisons, social workers, principals and guidance counselors, they know they can tap into these community groups, and get resources."

We found it astounding the number of immigrant-oriented CBOs that existed in every community. How did these CBOs fund their operations? One particularly knowledgeable community organizer and school board member offered,

> [Y]ou have philanthropy, local philanthropy, individual donors, fundraisers, breakfasts and different events where people raise money for your organization, you have corporate sponsors . . . [T]hey get money from, for example, the school system to conduct programmatic work in the school system . . . and they will get contracts from the city government, mayor's office, migrant ed.

Then there are national organizations like the ACLU, the Mexican American Legal Defense and Educational Fund (MALDEF), UnidosUS, Catholic and Lutheran charities, and immigrant and refugee rights organizations with which many of the districts have relationships. The codirector of a fledgling CBO dedicated to supporting undocumented immigrant students (ImmSchools) explained that being connected to large national organizations could lead to introductions to corporate donors and others willing to support smaller local organizations like theirs.

A major community-based resource that administrators in many of these districts mentioned was the church. Immigrant parents recognized the churches as places of safety and would attend meetings and go there for help. A southern superintendent explained how they handled distance learning during the pandemic with immigrant families that needed assistance:

> I'm working now with many of the local churches, minority churches, so I can provide Wi-Fi to them [immigrant families] . . . so, we've put Wi-Fi routers in buses and we're parking them in the church parking lot. So those are safe havens where the students feel very comfortable, and the parents do, to go into those churches . . . I've got a pastor group involved with that.

Some of our informants also noted the unique role of a local church as a community resource center for many immigrant families who need immediate support. Another southern superintendent recounted what he had observed in his community: "For our boys and girls here [who were separated from their parents due to ICE raids], I saw our people in our communities at churches gathering food, handing out food to kids." A southern educator also shared a similar experience: " [After ICE raids had occurred] . . . we moved to a Catholic church that had a community center. And we created a rapid response center . . . [W]e actually created a rapid response guide for other people to do this [how to respond to ICE raids]."

Strategies for Supporting Immigrant Students and Families

Professional development is a strategy that many districts reported using to help teachers and staff know how to identify problems associated with immigration enforcement stress and address it. This included trauma-informed teaching and basic knowledge of laws affecting students, such as *Plyler v. Doe* and *Lau v. Nichols*, both of which provide rights and protections for immigrant students. One northern superintendent was explicit about the critical need for professional development specific to teaching immigrant students: "[T]eachers know how to teach math but don't know about [immigration issues], they have background in math, language arts pedagogy, what they do not have background in is this."

After a raid that traumatized the teachers in a rural southern district, the very proactive ELL coordinator reached out to her district administration and said, "I'm going to have a meeting for educators, if you don't mind to send a text to them and see if they want to attend. And we'll see who comes. This is Saturday. I'm thinking, you know, I'll get ten people. I get a hundred educators in the room . . . I then set up a helpline for teachers."

There is an obvious need and desire on the part of teachers to access information about helping immigrant students with enforcement actions. Another critical goal of professional development that many administrators mentioned was helping teachers and staff to build trust with students. A principal in a devastatingly poor urban area in the West described how she worked with students to create videos about pressing issues they were experiencing, including fear of deportation, and then had teachers watch the videos to gain insight into what their students were dealing with.

Building trust with families was also seen as critical to these administrators. Especially after an incident with immigration agents, parents can be afraid of everyone, not knowing who is behind the deportation or raid. One southern superintendent who experienced this said, "Our main thing is we are just trying to rebuild relationships." A common piece of advice in this regard is to train the front-office staff to welcome parents when they come to the office. But this is difficult to do when no one in the office speaks the parents' language. In one southern district where none of the office personnel spoke Spanish, the ELL coordinator taught "cheat sheet" Spanish to the staff, including phrases like "Wait a moment, I will get the teacher for you." "Let me call you back." "Take a seat." Other trust-building activities included offering English classes for parents, and some mentioned advocacy training, especially for the parents of special education students advocating for services and understanding the Individual Education Plan (IEP). Some districts also explicitly welcome all students and families in multiple languages on their websites and list contacts for emergency health, food, clothing, and housing as well as counseling for trauma and information about immigrant rights. Such public and explicit support of immigrants, however, is mostly found in states with progressive immigration policies. Similar services were offered in districts in conservative areas, but the schools were sometimes less overt in advertising this. Of course, trust is best built through personal interactions, and in one southern district in a red state, the district arranges for all new immigrant parents to register for a *plática* (conversation) in small groups with other Spanish-speaking parents, where "they can tell their stories" and feel less alone in the new environment. In small districts with limited non-English language skills, ELL teachers and/or partner CBOs were charged with outreach to families and organizing support for them. In a small district in which the superintendent spoke Spanish, she met regularly with immigrant parents and was proud to say that parents called her directly with their concerns. There was no lack of trust. Even though it was a district that had been threatened by ICE, the superintendent was seen as someone on their side.

Providing accurate information about immigration laws and rights was also seen as important by administrators. Many mentioned the negative power of rumors, both in these interviews and in the survey we conducted. Rumors spread rapidly through immigrant communities and parents keep their children home out of fear, or avoid going to the schools for any purpose. As one state director shared with us, "It was really challenging to get . . . truthful information because our rumors were so pervasive, and I think it . . . spreads so quickly within the immigrant community that there's just a tremendous amount of fear." This adds unnecessarily to the major problem of absenteeism, so schools are anxious to dispel the baseless rumors. A midwestern principal also recounted his experience:

> We've had situations where a rumor is passing through the community and maybe a few people have been picked up very specifically . . . And we actually locked down our school at one point . . . We're not sending kids out unless we see their parents. So, we've had those things but that's been more on kind of word of mouth.

One way to dispel rumors is to provide accurate information for families. Immigrants' rights organizations have focused a great deal of attention on making "know your rights" materials available to other organizations, including schools. All of these districts reached out to parents about their rights, using these materials and calling on lawyers from community partners, including the ACLU. Most of these districts held organized meetings, often at the sites of CBOs or churches, where parents felt safe to attend. All of the districts represented in the administrator interviews engaged in informational outreach to the immigrant community, while the great majority of educators in our survey, which included twenty-four districts, noted that they thought it was very important to do so, but it was not happening. In one large northeastern district, informants told us that teachers were even accompanying students to immigration court.

Fundraising and providing basic necessities for immigrant families was also mentioned by administrators. All of the medium-sized and large districts in our sample had food pantries and clothing distributions and either had or made referrals for mental and physical health services. For immigrants in all these communities, the schools were the central institution where they could go for assistance of all kinds. However, a principal in a very low-income area in the West went beyond what we had heard reported in other districts. Acknowledging that many students were living in cars or RVs because they were homeless, she opened the school early every morning so the students could use the showers and bathroom facilities before school started. In one medium-sized southern district, the assistant superintendent described the "International Welcome Center" through which it funneled all new immigrant and refugee families to assess their needs, including food, clothing, housing, and medical and mental health services. The principal of a school in the Midwest lamented that "this state is very bad for immigrants," since the state did not allow any access for undocumented students to financial aid for college. So, the school began an annual fundraiser for this purpose a few years ago. The principal explained, "[W]e went from raising $7,000 the first couple years to around $80,000 this last year, and one of the ways we make it a big deal is . . . [we] communicate 'Hey, we do this because all of us matter.'" Again, this community in a very red state had taken on the immigrant students as its own, as an integral part of the community.

The superintendent of another medium-sized district in the South explained the services it provided:

> I have a whole migrant department. They go out and work in migrant areas. I send them out to inform, to give them support and then to determine what they need . . . and then they communicate it to the district. And then we try to make sure we are providing that . . . [W]e have a model that . . . brings in a lot of wraparound community supports . . . [W]e're able to get state grants, university grants . . . philanthropists and community members to join together to identify the needs of a neighborhood, of a school community. They are trying to bring in psychological counseling for students and their families. Free medical, dental and vision, so I'm making a clinic there . . . for the students, but also the school community, so parents can come.

The program the superintendent describes is the model of Communities in Schools, a nonprofit that operates in twenty-five states and the District of Columbia, which helps schools identify their particular needs, and then locates community partners that can address those needs. Its unique design is based on creating a suite of services that are customized to each school community.[3] It is aligned with a growing movement to acknowledge that schools alone cannot meet all the challenges brought on by poverty and segregation. The "Broader Bolder Approach to Education" is a campaign started by the nonprofit Economic Policy Institute to push policies that serve the whole child and all of their needs, in school and out, with the understanding that only in this way can the educational opportunity gap be closed.[4]

In smaller communities without a long history of immigration, such as in the New South, districts may not have the infrastructure in place to support immigrant families in an emergency. After an ICE raid, which left a number of children without a parent and a community in shock, a district administrator in a conservative rural area put the word out that they needed donations to help the affected families: "We received $30,000 in 24 hours and, overall, $120,000, and what we did was pay the basic utilities for the families for two months and $1,000 bond for twenty people. I think because people knew the families, you know. Like they've become part of the economy, part of the people."

For all the rhetoric about faceless "illegal aliens" that drives people to the polls to "build a wall," several administrators mentioned the seemingly paradoxical situation in which the red state communities find themselves. One southern administrator commented that, as a result of raids, businesses suddenly lost workers and, "without that worker or without that population doing those jobs, gaps have to be filled." Another superintendent from the Midwest added, "We are a very Republican state, very, very conservative state. I think what differentiates us from an Arizona is that the people [here] recognize that education is essential for community and state welfare."

College and university partnerships were another way that districts of all sizes gathered resources to support immigrant students. There are some things that institutions of higher education can do particularly, and sometimes uniquely, well. As one northeastern superintendent recounted, "I think our local universities were incredible resources to us. They often led trainings for us, many of the professors did, the researchers did, and they did it oftentimes pro bono, which was very helpful to us." Another northeastern assistant superintendent, in charge of ELL and immigrant students in a large district, said she connected with a local university's student group that wanted to work with the undocumented immigrant students to guide them on how to get to college. She also recruited faculty from the university to give monthly trainings in their areas of expertise, such as recognizing and addressing trauma in the classroom. The dynamic superintendent in a medium-sized southern district, who was building several programs for migrant students and families, was also getting psychology interns from the local university to help staff her counseling center, and faculty from a local technical college to teach parents English, and then hopefully direct them to technical training so they would be more employable.

Another way that districts partner with colleges and universities is to get bilingual teacher interns to bring more language skills to the schools as well as to reach out to teacher preparation programs to help train some of their teachers in ESL and bilingual methods. One of the southern district superintendents offered that they relied on the local university for mental health and pediatric care services in the aftermath of an immigration raid. Medical, dental, optometry, and social work schools are often willing to take some students as patients through their clinics, or even go to the school site when asked.

Consulates aren't located in every city, but Mexico alone has fifty consulates in the United States, and it has several in large immigrant states, like California and Texas. Some administrators mentioned their relationships with a Mexican consulate. The Mexican consular corps also have arrangements with some other Central American countries to receive and assist citizens of those countries where they do not have a consulate in place. The Mexican consulates can be a significant, and often overlooked, resource for schools. Some sponsor college fairs, including help filling out FAFSA forms. All freely distribute books in Spanish covering the K–9 Mexican curriculum, which students can use in the transition from Spanish to English instruction. Additionally, all are charged with at least three services: (1) organizing informational sessions for immigrants so that they know how to access resources and plan in the event of threatened deportation (e.g., who will care for children?); (2) provide legal advice, referrals, and help with documents, such as power of attorney; and (3) help DACA students to pay application fees. Additionally, each consulate has a rapid response team to respond to ICE incidents and an up-to-date list of CBOs that work with immigrants. Of course, all of this is in Spanish, which can be an important advantage.

All these forms of outreach and care for the immigrant students and their families tend to create a strong bond between most of the immigrants and the schools. To what extent these extraordinary efforts are common across districts in the United States, we do not know.

Strategies for Supporting Teachers

As we heard from many administrators, teachers in heavily immigrant Title I schools, where fear of immigration enforcement reigns, can suffer from secondary trauma syndrome. Unfortunately, this often goes unacknowledged or unaddressed, even in some of the districts that work hard to support their immigrant students. Ironically, some districts provided professional development to help teachers identify and address stress and trauma in students but did not provide the same for their teachers. In fact, few seemed to have considered the issue at all. (Perhaps if we had interviewed union representatives, we would have gotten different answers.) When asked if the district provided particular supports for the stress, worry, and additional workload that fell on teachers as a result of immigration enforcement activities, administrators either mentioned that teachers could, on their own, access mental health benefits provided by the district, or pivoted to discuss the training provided for teachers to support their students. They had given very little thought to addressing the specific needs of the teachers and the challenges they faced. And, not all districts provided mental health insurance.

Some administrators noted that they had teachers who were on DACA or who had undocumented family members, and the stress of these immigration situations was doubled in their cases. These teachers worried both for themselves and for their students. Even in these cases, it was not clear that a plan had been designed to address their situations. The focus was solely on helping the students and their families. One teacher/activist thought long and hard about the question of whether her district provided any support for its teachers and remarked,

> I think that would be a really powerful thing, to have someone to help process the things that happen. I've gone to, in the last ten years, six, eight funerals for students. I've gone to baby showers, I've held kids as they've found out their parents have been deported. Honestly looking back, it

would be amazing to have a resource, whether that's a small group or a person to process that, who is specifically helping me to process my job.

What Do Administrators Say They Need?

Before we concluded our interviews, we asked each educator if there was anything else they needed from the district or higher level. Here we list the kinds of things that administrators told us would help them to do their jobs in the face of immigration enforcement threats:

- Consistent with what we heard about the lack of direction or support from state departments of education on this issue, the administrator in a large northern district responded that they "need training on protocols—what to do if ICE shows up. Front-office staff, principals need the state department of education to come up with clear guidelines of what to do in various cases." The administrator felt the district was left to figure it out for itself, without the legal tools to do so.
- From the Midwest came a recommendation that the state department of education "strengthen ELL endorsements, with the idea that these teachers that are working with these students on the front line, that are hearing the most awful stories, have the ability, perhaps, to cope better because they have greater understanding."
- An urban principal in the West reflected on immigration policy and wanted to appeal to the government to listen to educators: "All kids in this country come through us, whether they are documented or not. They all have to come to school legally. So, if we are telling you, on the ground, what is happening to the kid, then we are the people you should be talking to, to find out how these policies are going to play out in the future."
- Another western superintendent from a rural area offered that they needed parent or community liaisons in every school "to keep track of children's needs."
- Mostly, administrators wanted more resources, social workers, counselors, and mental health professionals to support the teachers in working with students and families who are so traumatized by these immigration policies.

LESSONS LEARNED FROM DISTRICT ADMINISTRATORS

What did we learn from the many hours of talking with school administrators across the country?

First, contrary to what we had thought, the political slant of the state in which the district was located (red state or blue state) did not make much difference with respect to the support and services provided to immigrant students and their families. This appeared to depend much more on the local community and the commitment of the superintendent, administrative staff, and principals. Where administrators held the view that their responsibility was to educate *all* students (and we suspect this belief to be pervasive), they provided, sometimes quietly, the services that the immigrant communities needed to help ensure the students would stay in school and ultimately graduate. As one superintendent shared with us, "Our mantra is all means *all*. Every student that comes to us, regardless of where they're from . . . they get the very, very best that we can offer." This belief was consistent among all our informants. In states with progressive policies, the challenge was no doubt easier, and the resources more accessible, but state policies did *not* determine how these students were served. In one southern, very Republican state, administrators said rural districts that lacked services for immigrants would come to the large urban districts in the state to seek support, and these large districts were forthcoming.

Second, CBOs are critical resources for all districts, large and small, urban and rural, red state and blue state. All said it would be impossible for the school districts to adequately serve the immigrant community without the CBOs and other donors. One superintendent began counting them up and came to forty. All districts operate on a thin margin, and few receive funding specific to meeting the needs of immigrant students. The heavy dependence on these organizations points to the degree to which we underfund our public schools, especially in the area of social services and for low-income children.

Third, although administrators acknowledge the enormous stress that immigration enforcement creates for teachers and teacher turnover in the Title I schools is a widely recognized problem, relatively little attention was paid to the mental health and social support needs of teachers, even in districts known to be proactive in confronting the effects of this enforcement more generally. More than one district also had teachers on DACA, who at the time of the interview were at risk of deportation, and one of the principals worried aloud about the possibility of losing a DACA teacher whom she felt was an excellent educator. Although President Biden has pledged his support for DACA and reinstated it, it remains a short-term solution to a lifetime problem, which must be resolved. Even though informants noted the additional stress and anxiety felt by these teachers, there did not appear to be any further thought about how to support them. We found this curious and surprising.

Fourth, ICE activities have clearly terrorized communities and their schools, just as they have been designed to do. They represent a continuation of a strategy immigration authorities used throughout most of the last century and this one. However, these activities may have also had an unintended consequence. The sustained campaign of fear, and what increasingly has appeared to many otherwise conservative members of the school communities as unfair and counterproductive treatment of immigrants, has been creating a movement. As Ernesto Castañeda and his colleagues note, the social action of youth in support of DACA has been an important element in the Immigration Rights Movement.[5] Young people brought to the United States as children without agency, and educated here, are a very sympathetic group and, as such, have been able to gain a great deal of public support among both Republicans and Democrats to soften the hard edges of immigration policy. About 20 percent of those young people qualifying for DACA are also high school students—a large and vulnerable subgroup affected by immigration enforcement. These characteristics have moved them to the frontline of the Immigrant Rights Movement. They are the public face of all those young immigrants who work hard, study hard, and contribute to the nation. But as we found out, they are also the tip of an iceberg.

As we interviewed individuals across the states who had been dealing with immigration enforcement actions in their school communities, we uncovered a vast network of organizations that, on reflection, are more than partners with the schools. They are part of a national movement. These organizations, churches, philanthropies, CBOs, and national nongovernmental agencies (NGOs) not only provide services to the students, their families, and the schools, but often lobby local, state, and national policy makers on behalf of immigrants. While principals and superintendents may not be able to march and protest, they are often in alliance with others who can and do. The inhumane treatment of immigrants, and especially their children, has helped the Immigrant Rights Movement evolve from a focus on DACA as the primary policy goal to broader concerns, especially those things that concern children and, by extension, their schools.

Whereas, for many years, undocumented immigrants believed their only recourse was to hide in the shadows and hope not to be caught, the fight for DACA evolved to "Undocumented and Unafraid" campaigns in which young people "came out of the closet" as they marched in protest. The general public responded with a majority favoring legal status for these young people. But it soon became apparent that the DACA recipients were viewed as the "good" immigrants, while their parents were the undeserving immigrants. Yet it isn't possible to protect the students without protecting their parents, and this fact has fed the movement.

The immense pressure on the immigrant students and on their schools has turned the schools into key sites of organizing, although this is not always obvious. As some educators expressed, "We just reach out on behalf of the kids." But families know that the school is a safe place where they can turn for help, and schools are not without agency. The web of service providers for immigrant students and their families is often organized through the schools. Schools also adopt policies to shield their students and families from contact with ICE. It is nothing less than active resistance to these immigration policies because educators seek to protect their students. We see this in chapter 8 as the community school set up a legal clinic to advise and support undocumented students and their families as the school practices overt resistance to immigration authorities. Schools serving the children of immigrants have been under siege, but they may also be a political force in the making.

CHAPTER 8

Sanctuary Schooling

A Promising Model for Supporting Immigrant Students

KAREN HUNTER QUARTZ, NINA RABIN,
MARCO A. MURILLO, AND LEYDA W. GARCIA

THIRTY YEARS AGO, Donald Trump bought Los Angeles' famed Ambassador Hotel with plans to replace it with the world's tallest building. Using eminent domain, the Los Angeles School Board took the property from Trump and built the Robert F. Kennedy Community Schools to serve the local high-poverty immigrant neighborhood. When the school opened in 2009, no one could have imagined that Trump would continue to shape the property through his presidential policies on immigration. As one teacher shared, when "ICE was being very aggressive in the community, a lot of parents were afraid to take their kids to school." Countering this fear, the Robert F. Kennedy (RFK) Community Schools stood united—with the school district and state—in opposing the Trump administration's immigration policies. In this chapter, we share how one of these schools, the UCLA Community School, has established over a ten-year period a set of norms, structures, policies, and practices that provide one model of sanctuary schooling. We offer this example knowing that not all communities could or perhaps would even want to replicate our model, but that many policies and practices are transportable to other school contexts.

The UCLA Community School supports and encourages immigrant students like Pedro, a high school sophomore who fled his home country in Central America at the age of seventeen. At the school, Pedro participated in a special seminar for newcomers, engaged in open discussions of immigration policy in several of his classes, and formed supportive and trusting relationships with teachers and peers. All this eventually led him to disclose to a school administrator his fears about an upcoming hearing in immigration court that would almost certainly have led to his deportation, because his family had hired an untrustworthy attorney to represent him. Sensing his anxiety about initiating a legal consultation on his own, the school administrator personally walked him to a legal clinic on the school campus where he could receive help. In the weeks and months that followed, Pedro grew more engaged in school as his fears regarding the possibility of impending deportation receded. Now, with support from teachers and legal representation, Pedro is on a path to legal status and continues to work towards his G.E.D.

Pedro's story, described in more detail below, illustrates the potential of sanctuary schooling. In a time when schools, college campuses, towns, and even states have used the term "sanctuary" to express their solidarity with immigrant communities, it is surprising that the term itself does not have a clear definition. We offer one model of what a robust, multifaceted conception of sanctuary can signify within the context of a school district, city, and state that have also claimed sanctuary status. This means going beyond keeping ICE agents off the school's campus, although clearly this is one important piece of sanctuary.[1] We focus on the school's efforts to create trusting relationships and a strong sense of belonging where immigrant youth and families feel not just a sense of safety but also agency. This conception of sanctuary aims to counter the wide-ranging marginalization of immigrant youth and families in society by creating an equally wide-ranging set of institutional structures, policies, and practices designed to integrate immigrants as coequal partners in the school community and beyond.

Our chapter begins by mapping how and why schools have become a key site for today's sanctuary movement, and how these dynamics played out in the specific context of the UCLA Community School. We then describe four key steps the UCLA Community School took to create a sanctuary campus: (1) articulating a school policy; (2) creating safe and inclusive instructional spaces; (3) supporting meaningful family engagement; and (4) providing legal resources and support.

DESIGNING SCHOOLS AS SANCTUARIES

The sanctuary movement began in the 1980s, when churches offered shelter to Central American refugees in flight from horrific civil wars ravaging the region. The US legal system failed to recognize the asylum claims of these migrants and actively pursued their deportation. In response, a growing network of churches and synagogues offered the migrants sanctuary. In the renewed sanctuary movement of recent years, schools have been a natural locus of activity, serving two distinct subpopulations of immigrant youth. First, there are the "DREAMers"—the term used for young undocumented people whose parents brought them to this country when they were young and who have received all or most of their education in the United States. These young people tend to be completely acculturated to the United States and yet live with the constant fear that they and/or their family members could be deported to a country they do not know and the ongoing uncertainty about their legal status and future. Schools have become a key site where their vulnerability and the immense societal challenges they face play out.[2] Second, there are "newcomers," the term Los Angeles Unified School District uses to refer to any English language learners who have arrived in the United States within the last three years. Many of these students are part of a wave of unaccompanied youth and family units from Central America, who have fled the violence and turmoil in these countries in increasing numbers in recent years.[3]

In addition to these migration dynamics, the concept of sanctuary schooling is built upon the idea that "the fates of urban schools and communities are linked."[4] The community schools movement, set in motion more than a century ago by John Dewey and Jane Addams, embraces this shared fate. Community schools are "the hub of the neighborhood, uniting educators, community partners, and families to provide all students with opportunities to succeed in school and in life."[5] Marcelo Suárez-Orozco and

Carola Suárez-Orozco emphasize that "embracing and helping immigrant students to achieve their full potential is the educational challenge of our generation."[6]

The UCLA Community School was designed in 2007 to build on the assets of local students and families and meet a broad range of social, economic, legal, and educational needs.[7] Housed together on a historic site, the six RFK Community Schools share responsibility for an enormous twenty-four-acre physical plant that serves over four thousand students and spans an entire city block. Principals from the six schools serve on a building council that governs the site in accordance with a shared vision rooted in the social justice philosophy of the schools' namesake, Robert F. Kennedy, who was tragically assassinated in 1968 in the Embassy Ballroom of the Ambassador Hotel, now the site of the school's library. Kennedy's long-standing friendship with Cesar Chavez, Dolores Huerta, and other civil rights leaders is memorialized in this space in a public art mural by Judith Baca entitled "Seeing Through Other's Eyes." It is this social justice legacy and ethic of compassion that lays the foundation for sanctuary schooling at the UCLA Community School as well as the other five Robert F. Kennedy Community Schools.

When the UCLA Community School opened in 2009, students living in the adjacent neighborhoods moved to the school from over sixty schools throughout Los Angeles, ending long bus rides out of the community to find a good education. More than 75 percent of children (age seventeen and younger) in the school's neighborhood are in immigrant families (children who live with at least one parent who is foreign born).[8] The school's one thousand students are predominantly Latinx (81 percent), Asian (10 percent), and Filipino (5 percent), and most (92 percent) qualify for free or reduced-price lunch. One in six of these students was born outside the United States, most from Central America, Mexico, and the Philippines, and almost all students speak a language other than English at home. Class sizes range from twenty-two to twenty-five students in elementary grades to thirty to thirty-six in the upper grades. Thirteen percent of students are complex learners, educated in a special education inclusion program. Three administrators oversee a support staff of three counselors, one school psychologist, one psychiatric social worker, one coordinator, one ELL coach, a parent center representative, and several aides and paraprofessionals.

Becoming a sanctuary school has been a decade-long process. Since its opening, UCLA Community School has addressed immigration status at an individual and structural level to build trust between the school and students as well as parents. From ensuring that students could participate in an internship program without requiring a background check to helping undocumented students navigate the college choice process, the school's early years brought to the forefront the need to carefully consider the intersection between legal status and education. Over the years, the school has developed structures and systems to protect students' privacy when they disclose their legal status, seek guidance to attend college, and make postsecondary educational decisions. Through research and local partnerships, the school's work on immigration issues has evolved beyond college going to include wraparound services and supports that address broader needs related to legal status.

ARTICULATING A SANCTUARY SCHOOL POLICY AT THE DISTRICT LEVEL

Although the ingredients of a sanctuary policy have been integral to the UCLA Community School since its founding, it was the 2016 anti-immigrant rhetoric and policies of the Trump administration that led the school to a more explicit articulation of its stance. The process was set in motion when the Los Angeles Unified School District (LAUSD) board of education passed a policy resolution entitled *LA Unified Campuses as Safe Zones and Resource Centers for Students and Families threatened by Immigration Enforcement.*[9] A year later, in 2017, the Trump administration issued an executive order that threatened to withhold federal funding from cities like Los Angeles that implemented sanctuary policies to protect immigrants from enforcement activities.[10] Possibly as a response to the federal government's threats, or due to a change in leadership at the board of education, LAUSD passed a new resolution in 2017, with language from the California Constitution and the California Education Code guaranteeing schools as safe havens for learning, free of racism, and discrimination of any kind.[11] This resolution presented immigration as caused by "social, economic, and political factors . . . which result partly from U.S. government and corporate policies and interests."[12]

The 2017 resolution reemphasized that ICE presence near schools has negative effects for all students and mixed-status families, and compromises the primary mission of schools: to create a safe learning environment. In response, the district created a companion reference guide with definitions of terms, pertinent laws, education code, as well as a checklist for schools to follow in case of any ICE presence or activity at or near a school site.[13] The board resolution required the superintendent to ensure all schools became resource centers and included partnerships with community-based and legal organizations to sustain schools as safe havens.

INTEGRATING A SANCTUARY SCHOOL POLICY
AT THE SCHOOL COMMUNITY LEVEL

Equipped with the district's reference guide and checklist, local schools faced the challenge of operationalizing and crafting their own sanctuary status. This challenge was taken up by a group of students at the UCLA Community School, who participated in a citywide educational justice coalition called Students Deserve. Initially, students met through their local Students Deserve chapters to discuss how they were impacted by the draconian immigration measures. Students also talked to parents and held forums to ascertain the situation from those most affected. With the support of teachers and parents, students became familiar with the language and elements of the district resolutions and formed a coalition of parents, teachers, and students across the six-school complex to take action. Together, this coalition created the RFK Community Schools (RFK-CS) Sanctuary School Protocol that operationalized key aspects of the board resolution, such as devising a quick-response system and training of personnel across the six schools. The RFK-CS coalition held several meetings and engaged with the community to create a protocol tailored to the distinct needs of the RFK complex with its multiple entry points. The protocol opened with a definition of sanctuary, fittingly called Preamble, an allusion to the US Constitution and the rights therein:

> RFK Community Schools are committed to being a safe place for its students and their families in the wake of immigration enforcement efforts.

A sanctuary school is as strong as a school's organization. We believe it is important to be proactive in protecting and providing resources for our families. Our site, in partnership with community organizations and legal services, will be a refuge where families can seek safety, information, and resources if they feel threatened or afraid.

The RFK-CS protocol was divided into three major sections: (a) Safe Zone Protocol, (b) Resource Center Commitment, and (c) Fostering a School-wide Safe Zone Culture. The Safe Zone Protocol included prerequisites for implementation, such as a commitment from all six schools as well as the training of existing crisis teams and all stakeholder groups. The coalition also created preformulated letters for parents in case of ICE activity in the neighborhood. To move its plan forward, the RFK-CS coalition presented the protocol to the RFK-CS building council, knowing it would need the principals' support to train all the teachers from the six schools, campus aides, cafeteria workers, and custodians. Three points of contention arose in the course of these discussions.

First, the Safe Zone Protocol called for "higher security at campus entrances" and the allowance of "fleeing community members as part of a 'policy of temporary refuge'" into a designated area in the campus. The coalition's request focused on street vendors around the site, all of whom were parents of children at RFK-CS. The discussions involved visitor policies and overall safety. In spite of the evidence presented by the students, parents, and teachers regarding the high level of ICE activity in the neighborhood and its negative impact on the community, and the fact that the section mirrored the LAUSD board resolution, the principals were uneasy about enacting such a "radical" protocol.

Second, the Resource Center Commitments included issuing identification cards for parents. Administrators were unsure if they could create forms of identification for the hundreds of parents at the site. The RFK-CS coalition decided to let that request go unfilled as it felt other parts were more pressing.

And third, the RFK-CS protocol requested that school police make a statement—separate from the resolution—to reiterate their commitment to students and families as well as their position not to enter into any agreement with immigration authorities or agencies. School police did not want to make a separate statement and felt their position, as district employees, was already part of the resolution. The RFK-CS coalition felt a separate statement would assuage the fear felt in the community. This demand was not met, but the school police officer met with students on several occasions and attended Students Deserve meetings to assure students of the protective role of school police and their commitment to never cooperate with immigration agencies. More recently, in light of the Black Lives Matter protests, Students Deserve has been active in conversations to defund school police.

Despite these areas of contention, the council accepted the majority of the protocol. After a few more meetings, they slowly began to calendar days for the RFK-CS coalition to train teachers and staff on the protocol—a requirement of the district resolution. Once the trainings were underway, the response was overwhelmingly positive. Teachers at all sites were moved by the heart-wrenching videos and personal testimonies students presented during their training. Students also trained cafeteria workers and supervision staff. They attended coffee-with-the-principal meetings throughout the site to assure parents that their school was a true sanctuary, a safe haven for students and their families.

In addition, the schools agreed to issue explicit instructions regarding ICE activity around the neighborhood, which required school security to notify administrators, who "would mobilize additional security as needed to campus periphery, while seeking to verify rumors through contacting community-based rapid response networks. Security works to ensure that ICE activity does not spill over onto campus." The protocol specified that schools would be placed on lockdown given verified ICE activity; information would be shared with teachers and staff. Students would be allowed to check in with families, crisis teams would be activated, and legal service providers would be contacted to support families. Once the building council implemented these campuswide steps, UCLA Community School student and parent trainers visited every advisory in the high school to shed light on the detrimental impact of ICE raids on the community and explain the rationale for the protocol. These visits also included "Know Your Rights" trainings for all secondary students. One teacher expressed concern over the presentations because the stories felt too "real." Overall, students were not shocked by the accounts included in the presentations because those stories represented part of their lived experience. Seeing students lead the trainings and share important information was inspiring for the whole community and helped mobilize more members to join a neighborhood rapid response network called the Koreatown Popular Assembly. The school initiated a campaign to sign up parents to receive texts (available in five different languages) regarding ICE raids in the area.

Ultimately, the RFK Community Schools Sanctuary Schools Protocol operationalized and breathed life into the district-level policy. Led by a coalition of students, parents, and teachers, the protocol was a collaboratively crafted, sanctuary schools policy that was locally negotiated and set in motion across the six-school complex and its surrounding community.

CREATING SAFE AND INCLUSIVE INSTRUCTIONAL SPACES

Complementing the school's sanctuary policy, UCLA Community School has worked for over a decade to foster students' and families' sense of belonging and safety inside the classroom. Teachers have designed instructional units on immigration intended to foreground immigrants' humanity, migration stories, and cultural richness. For example, students in an English class might discuss the social construction of having "papers," while in their government class they will debate the contributions of immigrants to the US economy. In addition, the Spanish teacher might facilitate a discussion on ICE, asking students to critically examine its role in promoting a culture of fear in neighborhoods, as well as ways to challenge anti-immigrant systems. It is difficult work to bridge education and legal status issues, but as one teacher shared, "[T]eachers have to be very deliberate in creating spaces where students are encouraged to share their identity." In doing so, teachers affirm and honor community members' immigrant origins and prepare students to be active and critical participants in society.

Drawing on students' and families' funds of knowledge, teachers have developed classroom practices that affirm and acknowledge the intersection between immigration and education. Most classrooms are decorated with posters and signs that indicate educators' support for immigrants. Some have taken the initiative to learn about students' migration journeys and have joined a community of learners brought together by Reimagining Migration, a project that aims to build young people's knowledge and understanding of migration. Moreover, as a dual-language school, teachers embrace students' home language to enhance learning and build on families' linguistic repertoires.

Despite the heightened barriers to immigration, each year the school welcomes many newcomer students, some of whom arrive unaccompanied from Central America, are eighteen or older, and have interrupted schooling. In response, UCLA Community School created integrated and designated spaces to support newcomer students' educational transition. For example, the school has created a specialized seminar class for newcomer students. This elective offers newcomer students the opportunity to receive targeted academic and social supports. It is a safe space to help students acclimate to the school and their new country, while providing teachers the opportunity to learn about students' lives in their birth country and connect them to support networks. Throughout the semester, guest speakers share resources with students, provide one-on-one support, and talk to them about college and career preparation. Overall, the class fosters a community of learners with shared experiences, whose needs are at the center of the course.

UCLA Community School is one of a handful of span schools in the district and state, serving students from the ages of four to eighteen in transitional kindergarten through twelfth grade. This structural design decision was intended to foster trusting, long-term relationships with students and families and mitigate the risks of students becoming alienated from school when they move between different elementary, middle, and high schools. The TK–12 span also affords powerful opportunities for multi-age learning. For example, to honor students' immigrant status and to support their English language development, the school created an instructional unit for newcomer high school students to write and illustrate a children's book about their migration journey. Throughout the semester, students reflect on their migration journey, giving careful thought to the words and pictures they choose to include. Months of work culminate with a book presentation to fourth- and fifth-grade students. After the presentation, the younger students offer supportive and critical feedback, making recommendations on the story's flow and ways to enhance its illustrations. Many are also happy to share that they have family members with similar migration stories. This is one of many practices at the school that intentionally address immigration—providing a safe space for exploration, agency, and reciprocal learning.

Beyond the classroom, there are other instructional spaces that address the challenges faced by undocumented students. The college counselor, in collaboration with teachers, administrators, and community members, weaves documentation issues into college presentations and supports for students and families. School staff have learned to be sensitive and responsive to legal status issues and have been diligent in helping students navigate the college application and decision process. As a result, the school sends most of its graduates to college. For example, 100 percent of the class of 2017 graduated with plans to attend college and 86 percent enrolled in college the fall after graduation, compared with 56 percent of students nationally who attend low-income, high-minority schools.[14]

The story of Tania is one example of how the school's college-going culture supports undocumented students. Tania had been separated from her mother for a decade and traveled from El Salvador as an unaccompanied youth to be reunited. She kept to herself and had a difficult time adjusting to her new school environment. It took weeks for anyone to hear her voice, but it was evident in her journal entries and artwork that she was a budding artist and scholar. Tania enrolled in the newcomer seminar and shared her immigration experience being held for weeks in detention centers in New York and Texas, until she was finally released to her mother in California. Connecting with adults and peers at the school helped Tania find her way. By the end of sophomore year, she had straight As and was very interested in going to college. Tania graduated in 2018 and is currently a student at California State University, Los Angeles. Her dream is to become a therapist and help other immigrant-origin youth navigate their journeys.

Overall, the school's classroom practices and learning opportunities demonstrate a commitment to center immigrant students' assets, needs, and experiences as a core part of the instructional program. This work requires educators to take the time to know students as well as develop the expertise and sensitivities to address a deeply charged and emotional issue.

SUPPORTING TRANSFORMATIVE FAMILY ENGAGEMENT

A hallmark of community schools is their deep engagement with families, supported through structures such as parent centers, representation on governing councils, home visits, work opportunities, and extended learning programs. Transformative family engagement takes an asset-based approach—challenging the prevalent deficit-based ideas about families from low-income communities of color.[15] For example, parent leaders at the UCLA Community School conduct classroom observations, both to learn more about the school's instructional program and to share their feedback with teachers and administrators. They also analyze data on the school's progress and freely question particular educational practices. In general, teachers are open to these critiques and recognize parents as equal partners in the school community. The school embraces opportunities to support both parent agency and a sense of belonging and safety. To illustrate how the school has created safe spaces for immigrant families, we share the story of one long-standing afterschool program.

The Multigenerational Afterschool Arts (MASA) Program is held in a classroom each Wednesday, providing a creative, inclusive, and fun space for the school's TK–12 students, parents, and family members to gather. Together, they make art, build community, and honor home and cultural traditions. The program is taught by UCLA teaching artists, who work closely with MASA participants to co-construct meaningful learning opportunities. Each weekly session typically accommodates between thirty and forty participants, a large group representing a wide range of ages and artistic competencies.

The teaching artists are informed, sensitive, and creative in engaging families in art making to celebrate long-standing cultural traditions, such as Dia de Los Muertos, that tie immigrants to their home country.[16] For example, one of the mothers in the program shared (translated from Spanish):

> When I made the Day of the Dead projects, I honored my grandmother. In those projects, I remembered and chose to put things that my grandmother taught me, small things like this and that, but things I know that she liked and gave me. It is an honor to think of my grandmother this way because

it is an example of all the sacrifices she made and things that she has given our whole family.

Another parent discussed the complexity of honoring the home culture through the arts, describing an art project she first learned from her grandmother many decades ago, in a different country, as "bittersweet." While it is joyful to do the projects with her three children because "it helps keep us close as a family and a way to remember our history, and that makes me feel so glad," this mother described it as a sad experience because as time has passed, the loved ones she is honoring and their home country are both far away and long gone. Sensitivity to these complexities is crucial when asking participants to reflect on their families, childhoods, and home culture.

Community circles are a practice designed to create safe and inclusive spaces to share issues of concern to individuals and/or the group. Part of the larger restorative justice movement, these circles are guided by norms of trust that allow each person to express themselves. For example, on the morning of November 7, 2016, parents huddled in the school courtyard, talking and crying. One father told a counselor, "You know, I am not a rapist. I work hard, I love my children, I don't hurt anybody." Later that day, MASA participants gathered in shock and distress and formed a community circle to share their emotions about what the election of President Trump meant to the country, the community, and individuals in the room. There were a lot of tears and fears expressed by everyone, all ages. Sharing in this way gave voice to the collective anxiety and disbelief.

To allow for further dialogue and processing, the teaching artists introduced a "Community through Collage" lesson, in place of the previously designed lesson—exemplifying the type of flexibility necessary in culturally responsive pedagogy. As one teaching artist reflected, "I have noticed that the lesson plans are not the focus of this program, but are starting points for students to build on." The collage lesson required very few instructions and served as a way for the students and parents to continue sharing their feelings regarding the election, but through art making. Participants made two- and three-dimensional collages in response to the prompt: What does sanctuary mean to you? The collages were then assembled into a sanctuary quilt that felt as raw and true as the experience in the community circle. The quilt was later displayed in the school's Immigrant Family Legal Clinic, serving as a powerful representation of the community's commitment to supporting one another.[17]

As the MASA program example illustrates, sanctuary schools provide myriad spaces that affirm the identity and experiences of immigrant families and give them opportunities to participate in school as equal partners. These spaces are culturally sustaining and support parents to meaningfully engage in the life of the school. Restorative justice practices such as community circle extend beyond the classroom and school day, reminding all members of the community that they belong and are safe.

PROVIDING LEGAL RESOURCES AND SUPPORT

Another key component of the school's robust conception of sanctuary is the on-site Immigrant Family Legal Clinic. This unique partnership between the UCLA School of Law and the LAUSD opened its doors in January 2019 and undertakes three interrelated types of activities: community education, direct legal services, and policy advocacy. This three-part strategy recognizes that legal support is not only about ensuring that immigrants caught up in enforcement have legal representation, although this is a crucial goal of the clinic. In addition, the legal clinic seeks to build trust and empower the community by expanding the number of young people on a path to legal status, providing students and parents with legal orientation and information so they are less susceptible to intimidation and exploitation, and giving legal expertise and support to community efforts to advocate for more just and humane immigration policies.

The story of Pedro, previewed at the outset of this chapter, illustrates how these various components work together. As part of its community education, the clinic provides classroom presentations on a variety of legal topics, including a presentation to the UCLA Community School's newcomer seminar on the basics of the US immigration system for unaccompanied minors. The orientation emphasizes the importance of obtaining legal representation and describes various forms of legal status for which young immigrants might be eligible. After one such presentation, Pedro spoke to a school administrator about his personal concerns about his own immigration case, and she helped him make an appointment for one of the clinic's free and confidential consultations.

Identifying clients in this manner, through classroom presentations and school-based referrals, is a unique and powerful benefit of having a legal clinic integrally embedded in the school community. There are certainly other legal service organizations that provide representation to immigrant youth and families, but many young people may not connect with these organizations for a range of reasons. First, young people may not recognize the life-changing difference an attorney can make. In addition, they often lack the stability and resources to seek out assistance at an organization that is not already part of their daily routine. Finally, in some cases, like Pedro's, they *do* seek out legal assistance but fall prey to low-quality assistance or even outright exploitation.[18]

Pedro had arrived in the United States about two years before the clinic met him, after leaving his home in a rural community in Central America where he had been raised as one of eight children. His mother suffered from numerous health problems, and his father was abusive and violent toward her and his children. When Pedro was twelve, his father abandoned the family, and Pedro dropped out of school to work full-time. He got a job selling hand-bags in a local market, where he was regularly robbed and threatened by gang members, and sometimes stoned by local vendors who resented his competition. Meanwhile, although his father had moved out, he continued to harass and abuse the family. At seventeen, Pedro could not withstand the stress and abuse any longer and traveled on his own to the United States in the hopes of reuniting with an older sibling who had migrated several years before. Upon arrival, he was immediately apprehended by Border Patrol. After about three weeks in a detention center for unaccompanied minors, ICE released him to his sibling in Los Angeles. His sibling lived near the UCLA Community School and promptly got him enrolled in school. Meanwhile, his sibling also found him an attorney who charged thousands of dollars to prepare an asylum application, which was rejected for technical mistakes. Pedro had several hearings in immigration court. with the judge growing increasingly impatient.

In his consultation with the legal clinic, Pedro explained that he was nervous about the lack of communication or effectiveness of his attorney. The clinic recognized that Pedro had a strong case for a special visa available to young immigrants who have been abused, abandoned, or neglected by one or both parents. Pedro's attorney had not been familiar with this type of visa and had not taken steps to apply for it. Pedro had a tight time frame to get the application filed before he became too old to be eligible and before his immigration case progressed to the point of a deportation order. The clinic worked intensively with Pedro, aided by the convenience of its location in his school. Pedro, like many newcomers, juggled nearly full-time work with school, so the clinic's accessibility was crucial in getting the work done to file for the visa on time. Like nearly every aspect of the current immigration system, the visa process is backlogged, but while Pedro's application is pending, the immigration judge agreed to pause his removal proceedings, and he received work authorization.

Pedro moved from working for cash in construction to a restaurant job on payroll. Several weeks after the clinic filed his application, Pedro contacted the clinic for a new consultation. This time, he did not want to talk about his immigration status; he wanted to know if some of the treatment he experienced in the workplace was legal. Although the clinic did not find any legally actionable claims, it connected Pedro with a local worker center where he could consider getting involved in organizing alongside other restaurant workers for better working conditions.

Pedro's trajectory—from a seventeen-year-old on a path to a deportation order and/or life in the underground economy, to a twenty-year-old with a strong visa application pending, asserting his right to fair treatment—illustrates the way the clinic plays a critical role in the robust goals of a sanctuary school. Through a combination of presentations to students, parents, and community members on legal topics of relevance to the immigrant community, free and confidential consultations, direct legal representation, and engagement in local policy advocacy efforts, the clinic aims to further the school's broader goal of creating a place where students like Pedro are active participants and agents of change in their communities.

IMPLICATIONS AND CONCLUSION

This story of sanctuary schooling is a case study of policy making at a highly localized level. It offers an in-depth, on-the-ground examination of how one school interprets and enacts policies made at the district and state levels. We have looked inside the collective problem-solving process of a specific school, working to create a safe haven for immigrants in a particular community, at a particular time. We have heard about students developing sanctuary school protocols and training teachers, counselors helping meet college funding gaps for undocumented students, teaching artists and families creating sanctuary quilts, and school-based lawyers helping to change the life course of immigrants exploited within their own community. While it is common to acknowledge that context matters in social change efforts, it is rare to see the local as the foreground—what some have called "the new localism."[19] Espousing a form of participatory democracy, Bruce Katz and Jeremy Nowak have documented how cities create cross-sector and collaborative networks that "mirror the complexities of the challenges we face."[20] Similarly, we have tried to capture, at a micro-level, how local schools can create collaborative structures and practices that address the very complex challenge of educating and keeping safe immigrant students and their families.

We acknowledge that educators' ability to act and support undocumented immigrants are nested within distinct local, state, and federal contexts.[21] As such, while possessing a similar spirit to serve as havens for immigrants, sanctuary schools will look different across regions, and states. For example, in 2017 California passed Assembly Bill 699, which requires that all local educational agencies in California implement certain protections to ensure that all students, regardless of immigration status, have equal educational opportunities. Schools in the K–12 educational system in California (as well as New York, Illinois, and other states) are well positioned to curb xenophobia by creating welcoming spaces where students and families feel they belong and are safe. In contrast, schools in other states (such as Florida, Texas, and Georgia) will face significant challenges to local efforts because of state-level policies that seek to ban sanctuary policies and laws and, in some cases, even attempt through legislation or other agreements to require state and local government entities to enforce federal immigration laws.[22]

The United States remains divided on immigration policy and reform, although the 2020 reinstatement of DACA and the Biden administration's progressive legalization bill are signs that the tides may be shifting. This is good news because the evidence is clear that immigration status has deep and long-term consequences related to individuals' educational trajectories, well-being, and economic opportunities.[23] We agree with Leigh Patel, who argues that "[s]anctuary cannot merely be given or proclaimed as public rhetoric. True sanctuary requires much more furtive, strategic, and selfless behavior on the part of those who already enjoy the protection of walking freely in society."[24] Looking inside one school community's "furtive and strategic" effort to create sanctuary within an immigrant-rich central city neighborhood, we have argued for a multifaceted conception of sanctuary that includes but goes beyond policies that keep ICE agents off campus.

For schools seeking to become sanctuaries, we caution that it takes time and a strong commitment to developing trusting relationships over many years. We recommend creating local policies, protocols, and instructional practices that help all members of the community feel a strong sense of belonging, safety, and agency. Take stock of the myriad spaces that can serve as sanctuaries, including classrooms, college centers, afterschool programs, community response networks, and on-site legal clinics. Develop these spaces to build upon and sustain the many cultural assets of immigrant students and their families. In these spaces, we witness the amazing courage of those in liminal states of immigration, which inspire everyone in the community to a greater sense of what it means to be agents of social change. It is from this foundation that schools can create sanctuary policies, practices, and structures to support immigrant youth, their families, and their communities.

CHAPTER 9

Fear and Redemption

PATRICIA GÁNDARA

W HEN WE FIRST SET OUT to research the impacts of immigration enforcement on US schools, we were tempted to believe that what
was happening to immigrant students was the result of the unintended
consequences of harsh immigration enforcement that had not considered
the potential effect on these students. Yet, the more we considered the larger
context of immigration enforcement in this country over time and the way it
had evolved, especially under the Trump administration, the more we came
to believe that the impact on students was not an accident. Immigration
enforcement in the United States has always been driven by fear: both fear
of "the other" invading our land and fear instilled in immigrants of forever
living a shadow existence or being separated from loved ones. But the ugly
rhetoric of the Trump administration, calling Mexican immigrants rapists,
criminals, and "bad hombres," had raised the fear and social division to a
new level. There was a time when Hispanic immigrants were largely young
males without family members, living more or less invisibly in a few areas
of the country. But that time is long past. Now, thanks in part to Donald
Trump, they are highly visible and widely disparaged. Immigration authorities are acutely aware that these immigrant laborers (that the economy de-
pends on) are attached to families; ICE agents have waited outside schools

and near school bus stops, they have grabbed children out of the arms of their parents and put them in cages. Children have asked their teachers, "Why do they hate us?" And we have heard from educators that students who used to be detained for days in immigrant sweeps were now held in traumatizing lockup for weeks and months. In this way, the immigration authorities have ratcheted up the fear in the immigrant community to near hysteria. Surely, they know that children who are witnesses to and victims of these actions are also students—and they are tied to our schools. It does not take a leap of logic to realize this will have a negative impact on schools and the mental health and development of children. We have attempted in this book to call attention to the ways in which this reign of fear has been undermining the education of millions of students—mostly citizens but all deserving of schooling—and making it impossible for our most challenged schools to realize their mission of providing equitable educational opportunity. We therefore want to end this volume with a chapter devoted to recommendations for how we might redeem ourselves as a nation for the inhumane way we have treated these, our children. This is especially critical for the Biden administration, which has vowed to pass immigration reform. In the process of negotiating new immigration policy, it is essential to not forget the students, their teachers, and their schools.

If nothing else, the coronavirus pandemic of 2020 made clear the critical importance of schools in the lives of children, not just for academic learning but for general well-being. Mental health professionals have sounded the alarm about both the short-term and long-term impacts of the loss of in-person schooling on psychological well-being. They call out the depression, anxiety, and loss of motivation that may continue for years as a by-product of the absence of the stable, normal routines and interactions that occur in school. And this is in the best of circumstances, for children with at least one parent in the home, who have dependable food and shelter, who are not subject to abuse or neglect. For the children of low-income Hispanic immigrants, the impact can often be far worse. Because of the disproportionate impact on their parents, who not only are usually poorly compensated for their labor but are also often considered "essential workers" in high-risk industries (e.g., food processing) and services (e.g., hospital and hospitality workers), these children have been multiply disadvantaged.

They have had no parent at home to oversee their schooling. Their parents cannot afford to stay home with their children, unless they are laid off from their employment, which is also disproportionately the case for Hispanic parents, as demand for service industry jobs declined during the pandemic. Given that families in which even one parent lacks legal documentation are ineligible for any federal unemployment aid, when a job is lost, the family is often thrust into deep poverty. In this case, the stress can be so great that attention to schooling necessarily takes low priority, even if the home was equipped with a computer and reliable internet, and parents read and write English well enough to support their children's schooling. For most children of Hispanic immigrants, these conditions do not exist. Add to this the threat of immigration enforcement, and the impact on students can be overwhelming. We heard from educators *before* the pandemic that under "normal" circumstances of poverty and threats of immigration enforcement, high school students, even high-achieving, college-bound students would leave school before graduating, disillusioned by the uncertainty of their future. Many educators recounted the words of their students: "Why bother with school if we are just going to be deported?"

The constant threat of immigration enforcement appears to be pervasive among Latino youth, even those who are citizens and even those living in parts of the country where ICE is not very active. A recent study by the Migration Policy Institute, a nonpartisan think tank, found that more than half of Latino adolescents it surveyed in Houston and Rhode Island feared deportation of someone they knew, and many (12 percent) feared their own deportation, even though they were citizens. The anti-Latino and anti-immigrant rhetoric of the Trump administration has so pervaded the country that many youth see themselves as targets and change their behaviors (e.g., avoiding after school activities, driving less) as a result.[1] We discovered a similar phenomenon among Puerto Rican youth in our conversation with administrators. Even though Puerto Ricans are US citizens, many worried that their names and their language could be confused with non-citizen Latinos and put them at risk of deportation. For many Latinos in the United States today their ethnicity carries an unwarranted stigma of "illegality."

When, as we found, more than 80 percent of educators report their immigrant students overtly exhibiting fear and anxiety about the possibility of going home to find their parents gone, to the point of affecting their ability to pay attention in school, this is indefensible. When these students are bullied by their peers and told they are not wanted, "go home," "build the wall," this is indefensible. When students' academic performance is reported by their teachers to be declining as a result of fear and trauma induced by ICE threats, this is unacceptable. As a humane society, we simply cannot stand by and allow children to be treated this way. It cannot be stressed enough that these students are overwhelmingly US citizens (nearly 90 percent according to Migration Policy Institute) and refugees, as well as young people who have spent most of their lives in the United States and know no other country as home. The small percentage that do not have legal residency, or a claim to it, are nonetheless granted a free K–12 education by the US Constitution. Thus, all of the children of immigrants and refugees in our schools are legally and legitimately exercising their right to education. And educators are legally and legitimately providing that education to these students to the best of their ability. Nonetheless, immigration policies and anti-immigrant rhetoric under the Trump administration not only attempted to delegitimize this right but also so harmed the schools that serve these students and their peers, and stressed and burdened the educators who teach them, that an equitable education is simply not possible for many of them.

We heard, and read, heroic stories of courage and commitment to these students on the part of educators, and heartbreaking disillusion when students were swept away by family deportations or deprivation that was so great students had no option but to leave school to help out their families. As one superintendent reminded us, many of the teachers become a second mom or dad to these students, and they suffer when their students suffer. Just as it is indefensible to allow students to be treated in this way, neither should we accept the enormous burden placed on their teachers without extending support for them. We must find ways to support them if for no other reason than to increase the chances that they will stay in the schools that are a lifeline for the students and that are plagued by teacher turnover. This book is a plea to not look away, but to see clearly the damage we have inflicted on a generation of *our* students and the damage that has been done to the nation's collective future.

One in four children in this country today has at least one immigrant parent. Not all are living with undocumented parents and not all are poor. But two-thirds of Latino or Hispanic (the largest group by far) immigrant students *are* poor and attending underresourced schools that are struggling to meet their needs. This nation was founded and has been built by wave after wave of immigration, each wave considered to be "less than" the existing population—less smart, less ambitious, less able to fit in—and yet each wave of immigration has proven itself to be "more than"—more ambitious, more grateful for the opportunity to start over, and making new contributions to the nation. And each wave of immigration has, in fact, fit in. In this way, on the backs of immigrants, this country has achieved a remarkable and unique preeminent role in the world. But we should not take this for granted. If we shut off immigration, as the Trump administration attempted to do, we run the risk of undermining the economy because the native-born population does not produce enough babies to sustain it. When subsequent generational cohorts are smaller than the ones that preceded them, as has been the case in the United States for many years, the economy can shrink from not having enough workers and taxpayers filling government coffers that pay for the expanding needs of an aging society. Or, if we undereducate the immigrant students we have, then we are unable to fill the jobs that increasingly require more educated individuals. And, sadly, we betray the American Dream that brought these immigrants here.

What has given us hope and inspired us is the mobilization of pro-immigrant groups, many deeply connected to each other, working in every part of the country. It is clear that many have formed in response to witnessing the inhumane treatment of children, families, and schools caught in this terrible crucible. Communities that once espoused anti-immigrant sentiments are realizing that these immigrant youth are the sons and daughters of their neighbors and their children's friends. It was evident from the interviews we conducted that a movement is growing to undo the egregious policies in place under Donald Trump and replace them with more humane practices. We no longer need be the America of the nineteenth or twentieth centuries, using fear as a weapon against immigrants. And we surely should not be using it as a weapon against our students.

We cannot continue to witness what is happening to this generation of immigrant students and their schools and fail to act. These young people are our future, and our future will only be as bright—or as dim—as the education and nurturing we are able to provide for them. We are truly all in this together. As the result of the many dozens of interviews and thousands of surveys we conducted, and the companion research and writing of our colleagues in this book, we have come to a series of conclusions about what must be done to change course and preserve—and hopefully enhance—the assets of these children of immigrants in our schools. What follows are our recommendations, distilled from the data we collected on educators at all levels of the education system across the country.

OFFER STATE DEPARTMENT OF EDUCATION "KNOW YOUR RIGHTS" GUIDANCE TO IMMIGRANT- SERVING SCHOOLS

Every state department of education should provide basic protocols for dealing with ICE to every school district in its state along with a document that specifies the constitutional rights of immigrant students, both documented and undocumented, and the basic rights of immigrants as laid out in "know your rights" materials, such as those provided by the ACLU and many other organizations. Contrary to much public perception, almost all rights in the Constitution accrue to "persons," not "citizens." No matter what the politics of the state are, basic constitutional rights are the same across all the states, and immigrants retain many rights. Districts want to know what guidance they can share with their immigrant parents. State departments of education should be required to provide it.

OFFER WRAPAROUND SERVICES FOR CHILDREN IN POVERTY AT THE SCHOOL SITE

We must build on what we have learned from the coronavirus pandemic and immediately address the vast inequities we have seen laid bare in our society, particularly for our immigrant students and their classmates in Title I schools. In a wealthy and humane society, the current 8 percent federal augmentation to the budgets of these schools, attempting to meet the needs of students on the brink of homelessness, suffering food insecurity (as their parents cultivate and prepare that food for others), and wracked by fear and anxiety as they attempt to learn, is indefensible. Over the last many years, a movement has been growing that goes by many names: Broader, Bolder Schools Movement; Wraparound Services Schools; Community Schools. All are dedicated to remaking schools into one-stop community service centers for both academic and social needs, but struggle to hold the attention of the public. Given that the United States is unique in the first world in failing to guarantee basic social services, such as health care and childcare, and withholds basic government services such as SNAP from even legally residing immigrants, schools are the logical institution to take this on. School breakfast and lunch should be provided for all students in Title I schools (as well as students who qualify in non–Title I schools) without fearful immigrant parents having to go to the school and sign up. A hungry child cannot learn, nor can one read who cannot see the page or read the board. Medical, vision, and dental services as well as mental health and social services should be available in all of these schools. Currently these services are being provided by CBOs, other donors, and non-governmental organizations where they are available, but many communities are not connected to these resources. An enlightened and forward-looking society would invest in the children who are the emerging workforce that will pay for its social security and other government functions.

MAKE INFORMATION ON HOW SCHOOLS WORK AVAILABLE AND ACCESSIBLE FOR IMMIGRANT PARENTS

Programs like Parent Institute for Quality Education (PIQE) that provide training for immigrant parents, by immigrant parents, on how to navigate the schools and support one's children through the K–12 and higher-education systems, need to be part of the standard offerings in every school serving immigrants. [2] PIQE keeps students in school, connects immigrant parents to the schools, and is a trusted source of information and support because it is a parent-to-parent program. The federal government could easily sponsor this program or something like it in every Title I school serving immigrants.

ENGAGE COMMUNITY LIAISONS FOR BETTER COMMUNICATIONS

As a federal funding priority, every school serving immigrant students should have community liaisons assigned to communicate with the immigrant communities—to carry accurate information to them, to hear their concerns and communicate them to the school principal, and to help organize support for immigrant students. Many administrators mentioned this as a need that too often fell to the bilingual or ESL teachers who were in contact with these families. But that is two jobs for one person. In the era of fake news, it is also important to deliver accurate and reliable information through community liaisons to students' families who are often victims of unsourced rumors that can result in holding children out of school.

PHILANTHROPY SHOULD PRIORITIZE SUPPORT OF COMMUNITY-BASED ORGANIZATIONS THAT SERVE IMMIGRANT STUDENTS

Given that CBOs are currently carrying the burden of providing social and other services for low-income immigrant students and given the low probability that the country will immediately adopt a community schools model across the nation, philanthropy should be encouraged to prioritize funding that sustains the CBOs doing the on-the-ground work to support immigrant students. The many foundations that fund various aspects of school reform could make the biggest impact on schooling outcomes by helping communities to provide for the basic needs of low-income (immigrant) students and families. At the same time, it is essential that government play a significant role in ensuring the healthy development of children and the integrity of their schools.

UPLIFT SUPPORT AND CARE FOR TEACHERS

If we are to keep talented and dedicated teachers working with immigrant students in the schools that most need them, we must provide greater support for them. All DACA teachers should be immediately given a path to citizenship— they have more than proven their commitment to this country. Professional development in trauma-informed teaching practices should be provided for all teachers of immigrant students (as well as others who have experienced trauma due to the fallout from the pandemic). This includes practices like building a relationship with students so they know they can safely share their concerns in private; providing a quiet space to take a break for an overly anxious student; "checking in" with students daily to ascertain their emotional state; and making clear that the classroom (and school) are "safe zones" where all students are protected. It is also clear that these students will need extra time to make up for lost instruction. Federal Title III funding should be provided for this, in addition to Section 504 funds that can be used for tutors and counselors to help equalize these students' educational experience.[3] Helping teachers and counselors to meet students' psychosocial needs can reduce tensions and disruptions in the classroom and ease the burden on teachers.

For all teachers working with immigrant students, a community liaison could help reduce the load on them. Providing school staff accurate information about addressing immigration issues would also mean they don't have to spend their time researching this information.[4] But districts must find ways to support and reward their teachers of immigrant students with mental health services, small-group sessions to process their experiences during the school day, personal days to destress when necessary, and to further reduce the burden on teachers, appropriate and available referrals to support services for students having difficulty in the classroom due to trauma and anxiety.

COME TOGETHER TO USE OUR COLLECTIVE VOICES TO PROTECT THE CHILDREN OF IMMIGRANTS AND THEIR SCHOOLS

As a community of educators, we must lift our voices on behalf of the students. In the words of a principal with many students from mixed-status homes,

> The kids feel safe when they are with us. The problem is that their families aren't here with us. You know, their families are out there. So while the kids are in here feeling safe, they're worried about their parents . . . [W]e can't guarantee protection for their family. We can protect them while they're here. But if they are here and their dad is being deported, that takes away whatever level of safety they had, because now the safety is not about school. It's about whether they have a parent when they come back home.

Until we can solve this problem that haunts millions of students, they will never feel safe, and they will continue to experience the trauma we describe in this book. We can be supportive, we can—and should—bandage the gaping wounds, but we cannot heal the wounds when they are reopened daily. Educators have power. When they rise up with a single voice, they can insist that a festering wound that threatens our collective future be addressed. Educators can raise their voices against local law enforcement collaborations with ICE. Thomas Dee and Mark Murphy have demonstrated that these partnerships are terrorizing immigrant students and causing them to disenroll from school. School administrators can make their opposition known to such arrangements that have a negative impact on their students and their schools.

There is also broad agreement across the nation—and across political parties—in support of DACA or something like it, that protects individuals brought to this country as children and that also provides a pathway to full citizenship for them. Most people believe DACA makes perfect sense. A 2020 poll by the Pew Research Center showed that 74 percent of Americans favored DACA.[5] It should be an easy win, with a reasonable Congress that will put it to a vote. But it is not sufficient. At a minimum, that same attention and understanding need to be brought to the issue of children of undocumented or mixed-status families to protect them from losing their parents at least until they are able to complete their educations. The Biden administration has proposed a path to citizenship for the 11 million undocumented immigrants living in the United States today, providing they meet certain conditions. This would remove the onus on the children, and given the ability to work without fear of being deported, parents would hopefully be able to raise their children out of the dire poverty so many have fallen into as a result of the pandemic. But there is no certainty that the administration will be successful in garnering the needed support for this. One week into his presidency, President Biden was getting pushback both from the Congress and the courts for easing immigration enforcement.

It is critical that protections for the children of immigrants not be traded away in immigration policy negotiations. DAPA (Deferred Action for Parents of Americans), as proposed by the Obama administration, and struck down by the 5th Circuit Court of Appeals in Texas as an overreach of executive power, would have temporarily shielded parents of citizen children from deportation, allowed them to work legally and support their children, and brought stability and peace to about 5 million students. It is time that we redeem ourselves as a nation by making good on the promise of an equitable education for the children of immigrants, most of whom are US citizens. Continuing with policies of fear and intimidation of children is counterproductive to the welfare of the country and unworthy of a nation of immigrants.

NOTES

INTRODUCTION

1. Stephanie Potochnick, Jen-Hao Chen, and Krista M. Perreira, "Local-Level Immigra-tion Enforcement Policies and Food Insecurity Risk among Hispanic/Latino Children of Immigrants: National-Local Evidence," *Journal of Immigrant and Minority Health* 19, no. 5 (2017): 1042–1049, doi.org/10.1007/s10903-016-0464-5; Stephanie Po-tochnick, Jen-Hao Chen, and Krista Perriera, "Hunger in Young Children of Mexican Immigrant Families," *Public Health Nutrition* 10, no. 4 (2017): 390–395.

2. Luis Zaya et al., "The Distress of Citizen-Children with Detained and Deported Parents," *Journal of Child and Family Studies* 24 (2015): 3213–3223, doi:10.1007/s10826-015-0124-8.

3. The terms "immigrant children" and "children of immigrants" are often used inter-changeably, even though the children of immigrants are overwhelmingly not immi-grants themselves. One reason for this is that schools do not distinguish between the two and they are specifically required not to ask about children's citizenship status. We follow the convention of using the terms interchangeably, although where relevant we make the point that most are not themselves immigrants.

4. John Rogers et al., "Teaching and Learning in The Age of Trump: Increasing Stress and Hostility in America's High Schools" (Los Angeles: UCLA Institute for Democracy, Education, and Access, 2017), https://idea.gseis.ucla.edu/publications/teaching-and-learning-in-age-of-trump; Francis L. Huang and Dewey G. Cornell, "School Teas-ing and Bullying After The Presidential Election," *Educational Researcher* 48 (2019): 69–83, doi:10.3102/0013189X18820291.

5. John Gramlich, "How Border Apprehensions, ICE Arrests and Deportations Have Changed Under Trump," PEW Research Center, March 2, 2020, https://www.pewresearch.org/fact-tank/2020/03/02/how-border-apprehensions-ice-arrests-and-deportations-have-changed-under-trump/.

6. Amelia Thomson-DeVeaux, "Will The 2020 Democrats Reject Obama's Immigration Legacy?," FiveThirtyEight, July 31, 2019, https://fivethirtyeight.com/features/will-the-2020-democrats-reject-obamas-immigration-legacy/.

7. Jill Barshay, "Counting DACA Students," *Hechinger Report*, September 11, 2017, https://hechingerreport.org/counting-daca-students/.

8. Jie Zong and Jeanne Batalova, "How Many Unauthorized Immigrants Graduate from U.S. High Schools Annually?" (Washington, DC: Migration Policy Institute, 2019), https://www.migrationpolicy.org/research/unauthorized-immigrants-graduate-us-high -schools.

9. Julia Preston and Andrew Calderón, "'We Sit in Disbelief': The Anguish of Families Torn Apart Under Trump's Deportation Policy," *Guardian*, June 22, 2020, https:// www.theguardian.com/us-news/2020/jun/22/trump-deportation-policy-families -torn-apart.

10. Andrea Castillo, "LA Father Detained After Dropping Daughter Off at School May Be Deported," *Los Angeles Times*, July 17, 2017, http://www.latimes.com/local/lanow /la-me-romulo-avelica-deportation-20170731-story.html.

11. Ruben Vives and Andrea Castillo, "California, Trump Going Toe-to-Toe. Administration Officials Target State, In Part Because It's the Heart of 'Sanctuary' Movement," *Los Angeles Times*, January 21, 2018, B1, 5.

12. Carolyn Jones, "Immigration Crackdown Taking Heavy Toll on California Students," *Edsource*, September 28, 2017, https://edsource.org/2017/immigration-crackdown -taking-heavy-toll-on-california-students/588027.

13. Education Deans' Statement on DACA, January 18, 2018, Association of Jesuit Colleges and Universities (AJCU), http://www.ajcunet.edu/press-releases-blog/2018/1/18 /ajcu-conference-of-education-deans-statement-on-daca.

14. Kalina M Brabeck et al., "The Influence of Immigrant Parent Legal Status on U.S.-Born Children's Academic Abilities: The Moderating Effects of Social Service Use," *Applied Developmental Science* 20, no. 4 (2015): 237–249.

15. Throughout the book we use the terms "Latino" and "Hispanic" interchangeably, reflecting the ways different literatures refer to the Spanish-speaking population in the United States.

16. Hirokazu Yoshikawa, Carola Suárez-Orozco, and Roberto G. Gonzales, "Unauthorized Status and Youth Development in the United States: Consensus Statement of the Society for Research on Adolescence," *Journal of Research on Adolescence* 27, no. 1 (2017): 4–19, doi: 10.1111/jora.12272.

17. Jeanne Batalova, Brittany Blizzard, and Jessica Bolter, "Frequently Requested Statistics on Immigrants and Immigration in the United States" (Washington, DC: Migration Policy Institute, 2020), https://www.migrationpolicy.org/article/frequently-requested -statistics-immigrants-and-immigration-united-states.

18. Randy Capps et al., "Implications of Immigration Enforcement Activities for the Well-being of Children in Immigrant Families" (Washington, DC: Urban Institute and Migration Policy Institute, 2015).

19. Luis Zayas, "Disrupting Young Lives: How Detention and Deportation Affect US-born Children of Immigrants," American Psychological Association, 2016, www.apa .org/families/resources/newsletter/2016/11/detention-deportation.aspx.

20. Brian Allen, Erica M. Cisneros, and Alejandra Tellez, "The Children Left Behind: The Impact of Parental Deportation on Mental Health, *Journal of Child and Family Studies* 24, no. 2 (2015): 386–392, doi:10.1007/s10826-013-9848-5.

CHAPTER 1

1. Frank Luther Mott and Charles E. Jorgenson, *Benjamin Franklin Representative Selections, with Introduction, Bibliography and Notes*, in Project Gutenberg E-Book of Benjamin Franklin, 2010, https://www.gutenberg.org/files/35508/35508-h/35508-h.htm.
2. Peter Schrag. *Not Fit for Our Society* (Berkeley: University of California Press, 2010), 79–80.
3. Samuel P. Huntington, "The Hispanic Challenge," *Foreign Policy* 141 (2004): 30–45.
4. Schrag, *Not Fit for Our Society.*
5. "Still Searching for Solutions: Adapting to Farm Worker Scarcity Survey 2019," California Farm Labor Bureau Federation and University of California, Davis, 2019, http://www.cfbf.com/wp-content/uploads/2019/06/LaborScarcity.pdf.
6. Miriam Jordan and Santiago Pérez, "Small Businesses Lament There Are Too Few Mexicans in the U.S., Not Too Many," *Wall Street Journal*, November 28, 2016, https://www.wsj.com/articles/small-businesses-lament-there-are-too-few-mexicans-in-u-s-not-too-many-1480005020.
7. Brady E. Hamilton et al., "Births: Provisional Data for 2018," *Vital Statistics Rapid Release*, no. 7 (Hyattsville, MD: National Center for Health Statistics, May 2019), https://www.cdc.gov/nchs/data/vsrr/vsrr-007-508.pdf.
8. Josh Feldman, "Jeff Flake Responds to Trump's 'Unknown Middle Easterners' Tweet: 'A Canard and a Fear Tactic,'" *Mediaite*, October 22, 2018, https://www.mediaite.com/online/jeff-flake-responds-to-trumps-unknown-middle-easterners-tweet-a-canard-and-a-fear-tactic/.
9. While acknowledging that there are many avenues to enter the United States, such as through refugee status, usually from war-torn countries, and Temporary Protective Status (TPS), for those individuals from countries temporarily undergoing a crisis, this brief overview cannot accommodate an adequate discussion of the issues involved in these various forms of entry. This chapter focuses on events and laws pertaining only to immigration, both documented and undocumented.
10. Gabriel J. Chin, "The Plessy Myth: Justice Harlan and the Chinese Cases," *Iowa Law Review* 82 (1996): 151–182, 151–167, https://papers.ssrn.com/sol3/papers.cfm?abstract_id=1121505.
11. Leo R. Chavez, *Covering Immigration: Population Images and the Politics of the Nation* (Berkeley: University of California Press, 2001).
12. "Border Patrol History," US Customs and Border Protection, last modified July 21, 2020, https://www.cbp.gov/border-security/along-us-borders/history.
13. Since many (estimated at up to 60%) were born in the United States and some had never been to Mexico, these could not actually be repatriated to a place they were not actually from; however, the term was used euphemistically; Francisco Balderrama and Raymond Rodriguez, *Decade of Betrayal* (Albuquerque: University of New Mexico Press, 2006).
14. Adam Goodman, *The Deportation Machine. America's Long History of Expelling Immigrants* (Princeton, NJ: Princeton University Press, 2020), 40–46.
15. Goodman, *Deportation Machine.*

16. Goodman, *Deportation Machine*, 49–50.
17. "Number of Immigrants and Immigrants as Percentage of the U.S. Population, 1850 to 2018," Migration Policy Institute, n.d., https://www.migrationpolicy.org/programs /migration-data-hub.
18. Most Hispanics/Latinos at the time were of Mexican origin; however, Hispanic subgroups were not broken out.
19. Goodman, *Deportation Machine*.
20. Goodman, *Deportation Machine*, 107.
21. Goodman, *Deportation Machine*, 108.
22. Faye Hipsman and Doris Meissner, "Immigration in the United States: New Economic, Social, Political Landscapes with Legislative Reform on the Horizon," Migration Policy Institute, April 16, 2013, https://www.migrationpolicy.org/article/immigration-united -states-new-economic-social-political-landscapes-legislative-reform.
23. Douglas Massey, Jorge Durand, and Karen Pren, "Why Border Enforcement Backfired," *American Journal of Sociology* 121, no. 5 (2016): 1557.
24. Krishnadev Calamur, "The Real Immigration Crisis Isn't On The Southern Border," *Atlantic*, April 19, 2019, https://www.theatlantic.com/international/archive/2019/04 /real-immigration-crisis-people-overstaying-their-visas/587485.
25. Jens Manuel Krogstad, Jeffrey S. Passel, and D'Vera Cohn, "5 Facts About Illegal Immigration in the U.S.," *Fact Tank*, Pew Research Center, June 12, 2019, https://www .pewresearch.org/fact-tank/2019/06/12/5-facts-about-illegal-immigration-in-the-u-s/.
26. A. DeVeaux, "Will The 2020 Democrats Reject Obama's Immigration Legacy?," *FiveThirtyEight*, June 31, 2019, https://fivethirtyeight.com/features/will-the-2020 -democrats-reject-obamas-immigration-legacy/.
27. Steven L. Schlossman, "Is There an American Tradition of Bilingual Education? German in the Public Elementary Schools, 1840-1919," *American Journal of Education* 91, no. 2 (1983): 139–186.
28. Meyer v. State of Nebraska, 262 U.S. 390, 1923. Legal Information Institute, Cornell Law School, https://www.law.cornell.edu/supremecourt/text/262/390.
29. Aimee Eng and Daniel McFarland, "The Japanese Question: San Francisco Education in 1906," GSE Case Library, Stanford University, Case 2006-3, https://caselib.stanford .edu/case/2006-03.
30. Alex Nowrasteh, "The Failure of the Americanization Movement," *Cato at Liberty Blog*, December 18, 2014, https://www.cato.org/blog/failure-americanization-movement.
31. Zevi Gutfreund, *Speaking American. Language Education and Citizenship in Twentieth Century Los Angeles* (Norman: University of Oklahoma Press, 2019).
32. It is important to note that there was a long-standing problem of inadequate education of Spanish-speaking children in the Southwest, in large part the legacy of the Mexican-American war that resulted in Mexico losing a third of its land mass in 1848, and the incorporation of Mexican families into the US. This was especially egregious in Texas, where most Mexican children weren't able to access any education beyond primary grades, if that, well into the middle of the twentieth century. See Thomas P. Carter, *Mexican Americans in School: A History of Educational Neglect* (New York: College Entrance Examination Board, 1970).

33. "Children in Immigrant Families, 1990-2018," Migration Policy Institute, n.d., https://www.migrationpolicy.org/programs/data-hub/charts/children-immigrant -families; Randolph Capps et al., "The New Demography of America's Schools: Immigration and the No Child Left Behind Act," The Urban Institute, September 30, 2005, https://www.urban.org/research/publication/new-demography-americas-schools.

34. See Schools and Academies, Internationals Network, http://internationalsnps.org /schools/.

35. See, for example, Randy Capps et al., "Implications of Immigration Enforcement Activities for the Well-being of Children in Immigrant Families," Urban Institute and Migration Policy Institute, September 2015, https://www.migrationpolicy.org /research/implications-immigration-enforcement-activities-well-being-children -immigrant-families.

36. Grace Kao and Marta Tienda, "Optimism and Achievement: The Educational Performance of Immigrant Youth," *Social Science Quarterly* 76, no. 1 (March 1995): 1–19; Carola and Marcelo Suárez-Orozco, *Transformations: Immigration, Family Life and Achievement Motivation Among Latino Adolescents* (Palo Alto, CA: Stanford University Press, 1995).

37. Plyler v. Doe, 457 U.S. 202 (1982): 216, Justia Legal Resources, https://supreme .justia.com/cases/federal/us/457/202/#tab-opinion-1954578.

38. Migration Policy Institute DACA Data Hub, 2020, https://www.migrationpolicy.org /programs/data-hub/deferred-action-childhood-arrivals-daca-profiles; Julia Preston and Andrew Calderón, "'We Sit In Disbelief': The Anguish of Families Torn Apart Under Trump's Deportation Policy," *Guardian*, June 22, 2020, https://www.the guardian.com/us-news/2020/jun/22/trump-deportation-policy-families-torn-apart.

39. Numerous polls have been done on this issue and none shows lower than about 70% of people responding support DACA. This is true even among Trump supporters.

40. Leila Rafei, "Family Separations Two Years After Ms. L.," *American Civil Liberties Union News and Commentary*, February 26, 2020, https://www.aclu.org/news /immigrants-rights/family-separation-two-years-after-ms-l/.

41. Randolph Capps, Julia Gelatt, and Mark Greenberg, "The Public Charge Rule: Broad Impacts, But Few Will Be Denied Green Cards Based on Actual Use," *Migration Policy Institute Commentaries*, March 2020, https://www.migrationpolicy.org/news/public -charge-denial-green-cards-benefits-use, 2020.

42. Preston and Calderón, "'We Sit In Disbelief.'"

43. Andri Chassamboulli and Giovanni Peri, "The Labor Market Effects of Reducing the Number of Illegal Immigrants" (Working Paper No. 19932, National Bureau of Economic Research), https://www.nber.org/papers/w19932.pdf.

CHAPTER 2

1. Migration Policy Institute, "Children in Immigrant Families, 1990–2018," n.d., https://www.migrationpolicy.org/programs/data-hub/charts/children-immigrant -families.

2. The survey data covered the following states (numbers in parentheses show the number of participants for each state): Arizona (562), California (2,313), Florida (72),

Georgia (30), Indiana (358), Maryland (357), Massachusetts (139), Nebraska (209), New Jersey (231), New York (71), Oregon (341), Tennessee (314), and Texas (320).

3. Stephania Taladrid, "The Risks Undocumented Workers Are Facing During the COVID-19 Pandemic," *New Yorker,* April 13, 2020, https://www.newyorker.com /news/video-dept/the-risks-undocumented-workers-are-facing-during-the-covid -19-pandemic.

4. We acknowledge the limitation of the use of Hispanic students as a proxy for immigrant students since a wide variety of diversity exists among immigrant populations. We also recognize that the diversity among students from immigrant homes has been growing over the past decades. We also acknowledge that English language learner status can be a reasonably good proxy for child of immigrants. However, the label goes away when the students transition to fluent English, so it is an unstable indicator. Thus, due to realistic limitations of data availability, we used the share of Hispanics for this study.

5. Not all survey participants identified their school information, but the shares of the respondents from Groups 1, 2, and 3 are 15%, 29%, and 56% of the total participants, respectively.

6. National Center for Education Statistics, Public Elementary/Secondary School Universe Survey Data for the 2015–16 School Year, 2018, https://nces.ed.gov/ccd /pubschuniv.asp; NCES, Restricted-Use Civil Rights Data Collection (CRDC) for the 2015–16 School Year, 2018.

7. The detailed information regarding analytical methods for this study can be found in: Jongyeon Ee and Patricia Gándara, "The Impact of Immigration Enforcement on the Nation's Schools," *American Educational Research Journal* 57, no. 2 (April 2020): 840–871, doi:10.3102/0002831219862998.

8. See Ee and Gándara, "The Impact of Immigration Enforcement on the Nation's Schools," for more methodological details.

9. Ron Avi Astor, Heather Ann Meyer, and Ronald O. Pitner, "Elementary and Middle School Students' Perceptions of Violence-Prone School Subcontexts," *The Elementary School Journal* 101, no. 5 (2001): 511–528; Stephanie Kasen et al., "The Effects of School Climate on Changes in Aggressive and Other Behaviors Related to Bullying," in *Bullying in American schools: A Social-Ecological Perspective on Prevention and Intervention,* ed. Dorothy L. Espelage and Susan M. Swearer (New York: Routledge, 2004), 187–210; Stuart W. Twemlow et al., "Creating a Peaceful School Learning Environment: A Controlled Study of an Elementary School Intervention to Reduce Violence," *American Journal of Psychiatry* 158, no. 5 (2001): 808–810.

10. "Demographic and Economic Trends in Urban, Suburban and Rural Communities," Pew Research Center, May 22, 2018, https://www.pewsocialtrends.org/2018/05/22 /demographic-and-economic-trends-in-urban-suburban-and-rural-communities/.

11. Leif Jensen, "New Immigrant Settlements in Rural America: Problems, Prospects, and Policies," Carsey Institute, 2006; Olugbenga Ajilore and Zoe Willingham, "Redefining Rural America," Center for American Progress, 2019, https://www.americanprogress .org/issues/economy/reports/2019/07/17/471877/redefining-rural-america/; Silva Mathema, Nicole Prchal Svajlenka, and Anneliese Hermann, "Revival and

Opportunity," Center for American Progress, 2018, https://www.americanprogress
.org/issues/immigration/reports/2018/09/02/455269/revival-and-opportunity/.

12. "U.S. Immigrant Population by State and County, 2014–2018," Migration Policy Institute, https://www.migrationpolicy.org/programs/data-hub/charts/us-immigrant
-population-state-and-county.

13. Carolyn Saarni, *The Development of Emotional Competence* (New York: Guilford Press, 1999), 131–161.

CHAPTER 3

1. "Children in U.S. Immigrant Families," Migration Policy Institute, n.d., https://www
.migrationpolicy.org/programs/data-hub/charts/children-immigrant-families?width
=900&height=850&iframe=true; "Back to School Statistics," National Center for Education Statistics, n.d., https://nces.ed.gov/fastfacts/display.asp?id=372.

2. Douglas Massey, Jorge Durand, and Nolan J. Malone, *Beyond Smoke and Mirrors: Mexican Immigration in an Era of Economic Integration* (New York: Russell Sage, 2003).

3. Grace Kao and Marta Tienda, "Optimism and Achievement: The Educational Performance of Immigrant Youth," *Social Science Quarterly* 76. No. 1 (1995):1–19, http://
www.jstor.org/stable/44072586; Carola Suárez Orozco and Marcelo Suarez-Orozco, *Transformations: Immigration, Family Life and Achievement Motivation among Latino Adolescents* (Palo Alto, CA: Stanford University Press, 1995).

4. Donald J. Hernandez, Nancy Denton, and Suzanne McCartney, "School Age Children in Immigrant Families: Challenge and Opportunities for America's Future," *Teachers College Record* 111, no. 3 (2009): 616–668.

5. Stephanie Potochnick, Jen Hao Chen, and Krista Perriera, "Local-Level Immigration Enforcement and Food Insecurity Risk among Hispanic Immigrant Families with Children: National-Level Evidence." *Journal of Immigrant and Minority Health* 19, 5 (2017): 1042–1049, doi: 10.1007/s10903-016-0464-5.

6. Christopher B. Swanson and Barbara Schneider, "Students on the Move: Residential and Educational Mobility in America's Schools," *Sociology of Education* 72, no. 1 (1999): 54–67.

7. Robert K. Ream, *Uprooting Children. Mobility, Social Capital and Mexican American Underachievement* (New York: LBF Publishers, 2005).

8. Kelley Whitener et al., "Decade of Success for Latino Children's Health Now in Jeopardy," Georgetown University Health Policy Institute, May 2020, 5.

9. Samantha Artiga and Maria Diaz, "Health Coverage and Care of Undocumented Immigrants," Kaiser Family Foundation, July 2019, http://files.kff.org/attachment
/Issue-Brief-Health-Coverage-and-Care-of-Undocumented-Immigrants; the public charge rule is discussed briefly in chapter 2. It refers to a Trump administration policy to potentially deny legal resident status (green card) to any immigrant accessing federal programs or benefits.

10. Childtrends, "Preschool and Pre-Kindergarten," 2019, Appendix 1.

11. Patricia Gándara, "The Students We Share: Falling Through the Cracks on Both Sides of the US-Mexico Border," *Ethnic and Racial Studies* 43, nos. 1 and 2 (2020): 38–59.

12. Gándara, "The Students We Share."

13. Mark Dynarski and Kirsten Kainz, "Why Federal Spending on Disadvantaged Students (Title I) Doesn't Work," *Evidence Speaks*, The Brookings Institution, 2015, https://www.brookings.edu/research/why-federal-spending-on-disadvantaged-students-title-i-doesnt-work/.

14. Sean F. Reardon, "The Widening Academic Achievement Gap Between the Rich and the Poor: New Evidence and Possible Explanations" (Palo Alto, CA: Stanford University, 2011).

15. "Education Department Budget History Table: FY 1980—FY 2019 President's Budget," Budget History Tables, US Department of Education, October 26, 2018, https://www2.ed.gov/about/overview/budget/history/edhistory.pdf.

16. "Title III Part A Programs—Strengthening Institutions," US Department of Education, September 2020, https://www2.ed.gov/programs/iduestitle3a/index.html.

17. Andrew Reschovsky, "The Future of U.S. Public School Revenue from the Property Tax," Lincoln Institute, 2017, https://www.lincolninst.edu/publications/articles/future-us-public-school-revenue-property-tax.

18. Lorraine M. McDonnell, "Stability and Change in Title I Testing Policy," *Russell Sage Foundation Journal of the Social Sciences* 1, no. 3 (2015):170–186, doi: 10.7758/RSF.2015.1.3.0.

19. Jay Heubert, *High Stakes: Testing for Tracking, Promotion and Graduation* (Washington, DC: National Academy Press, 1999); Daniel Koretz, *The Testing Charade: Pretending to Make Schools Better* (Chicago: University of Chicago Press, 2017).

20. Patricia Gándara, "Charting the Relationship of English Learners and the ESEA: One Step Forward and Two Steps Back," *Russell Sage Foundation Journal of the Social Sciences* 1, no. 3 (2015):112–128.

21. Elizabeth U. Cascio and Sarah Reber, "The Poverty Gap in School Spending Following the Introduction of Title I," *American Economic Review* 103, no. 3 (2013): 423–427, doi: 10.1257/aer.103.3.423.

22. James Coleman et al., "Equality of Educational Opportunity," US Department of Health, Education and Welfare, 1966, https://files.eric.ed.gov/fulltext/ED012275.pdf.

23. Coleman et al., "Equality," 28.

24. David A. Gamson, Kathryn A. McDermott, and Douglas S. Reed, "The Elementary and Secondary Education Act at Fifty: Aspirations, Effects, and Limitations," *Russell Sage Foundation Journal of the Social Sciences* 1, no. 3 (2015): 1–29, doi: https://doi.org/10.7758/RSF.2015.1.3.01.

25. Erica Frankenberg et al., *Harming our Common Future: America's Segregated Schools 65 Years after Brown* (Los Angeles: UCLA Civil Rights Project, 2019); Gary Orfield and Jongyeon Ee, *Segregating California's Future: Inequality and Its Alternative, 60 Years After Brown v. Board of Education* (Los Angeles: UCLA Civil Rights Project, 2014).

26. Desiree Carver-Thomas and Linda Darling-Hammond, "Addressing California's Growing Teacher Shortage," Learning Policy Institute, 2017; E. García and E. Weiss, "Low Relative Pay and High Incidence of Moonlighting Play a Role in the Teacher Shortage, Particularly in High-Poverty Schools," Third Report In "The Perfect Storm in the Teacher Labor Market" Series, Economic Policy Institute, 2019; E. García and E. Weiss, "The Teacher Shortage Is Real, Large and Growing, and Worse than We Thought," First Report in "The Perfect Storm in the Teacher Labor Market" Series,

Economic Policy Institute, 2019; Samuel W. Flynt and Rhonda Collins Morton, "The Teacher Shortage in America: Pressing Concerns," *National Forum of Teacher Education Journal* 19, no. 3 (2009): 1–5; Elizabeth I. Rivera Rodas, "Separate and Unequal—Title I and Teacher Quality," *Education Policy Analysis Archives* 27, no. 14 (2019).

27. Linda Darling-Hammond, "Inequality in Teaching and Schooling: How Opportunity Is Rationed to Students of Color in America," in *The Right Thing to Do, The Smart Thing to Do,* ed. Brian D. Smedley et al. (Institute of Medicine, 2001), 208–233.

28. Darling-Hammond, "Inequality"; Karolyn Tyson, "Tracking Segregation, and the Opportunity Gap," *Closing the Opportunity Gap: What America Must Do to Give Every Child an Even Chance* (New York: Oxford University Press, 2013), 169–180.

29. See, for example, Niu Gao, Lunna Lopes, and Grace Lee, "California's Graduation Requirements," Public Policy Institute for California, November 2017; Edwin C. Darden and Elizabeth Cavendish, "Achieving Resource Equity Within a Single School District: Erasing the opportunity gap by examining school board decisions," *Education and Urban Society* 44, no. 1 (2012): 61–82, doi: 10.1177/0013124510380912; Darling-Hammond, "Inequality"; Alfinio Flores, "Examining Disparities in Mathematics Education: Achievement Gap or Opportunity Gap?," *High School Journal* 91, no. 1 (2007): 29–42, http://www.jstor.com/stable/40367921.

30. Robert Balfanz and Vaughan Byrnes, "The Importance of Being in School: A Report on Absenteeism in the Nation's Public Schools," *Education Digest* 78, no. 2 (2012): 4; Adrienne Ingrum, "High School Dropout Determinants: The Effect of Poverty and Learning Disabilities," *Park Place Economist* 14, no. 1 (2006): 72–79; Misty Lacour and Laura D. Tissington, "The Effects of Poverty on Academic Achievement," *Educational Research and Reviews* 6, no. 7 (2011): 522–527; Magnus Lofstrom, "Why are Hispanic and African-American Dropout Rates so High?" (working paper, IZA, no. 3265), http://dx.doi.org/10.1111/j.0042-7092.2007.00700.x.

31. Organization of Economic Cooperation and Development (OECD), "Helping Immigrant Students to Succeed at School—and Beyond," 2015, 9, Figure 6.

32. Frankenberg et al., "Harming Our Common Future"; Gary Orfield and Chung Mei Lee, "Why Segregation Matters" (Los Angeles: Civil Rights Project, 2005), https://civilrightsproject.ucla.edu/research/k-12-education/integration-and-diversity/why-segregation-matters-poverty-and-educational-inequality.

33. Russell W. Rumberger and Patricia Gándara, "Resource Needs for Educating Linguistic Minority Students," in *Handbook of Research in Education and Finance Policy,* ed. Helen F. Ladd and Margaret E. Goertz (New York: Routledge, 2015), 585–606.

34. "English Language Learners in Public Schools," National Center for Education Statistics (NCES), May 2020, https://nces.ed.gov/programs/coe/indicator_cgf.asp.

35. NCES, "English Language."

36. NCES, "English Language."

37. We follow the NCES's definition regarding poverty schools. In high-poverty schools, over 75 percent of the students are eligible for free or reduced-price lunch (FRPL); mid-high poverty schools are those where 50.1 to 75.0 percent of the students are eligible for FRPL; mid-low poverty schools enroll 25.1 to 50.0 percent FRPL students; and low-poverty schools have 25 percent or less FRPL students.

38. Hedy N. Chang and Mariajosé Romero, "Present, Engaged, and Accounted for: The Critical Importance of Addressing Chronic Absence in the Early Grades. Report," National Center for Children in Poverty, 2008, https://files.eric.ed.gov/fulltext /ED522725.pdf; Stacy B. Ehrlich et al., "Preschool Attendance in Chicago Public Schools: Relationships with Learning Outcomes and Reasons for Absences," University of Chicago Consortium on Chicago School Research, 2014, https://files.eric .ed.gov/fulltext/ED553158.pdf; Michael A. Gottfried, "Chronic Absenteeism and Its Effects on Students' Academic and Socioemotional Outcomes," *Journal of Education for Students Placed at Risk (JESPAR)* 19, no. 2 (2014): 53–75, doi: 10.1080/10824669.2014.962696.

39. Jens Manuel Krogstad, Ana Gonzalez-Barrera, and Luis Noe-Bustamante, "U.S. Latinos among Hardest Hit by Pay Cuts, Job Losses Due to Coronavirus," Pew Research, Fact Tank, April 12, 2020; Libby Pier et al., "COVID-19 and the Educational Equity Crisis Evidence on Learning Loss from the CORE Data Collaborative," Policy Analysis for California Education, January 25, 2021.

40. Parent Institute for Quality Education (PIQE), "Lifting up Voices," https://www.piqe .org/wp-content/uploads/2020/05/FINAL-LIFTING-UP-VOICES.pdf.

41. Jorg M. Fegert et al., "Challenges and Burden of the Coronavirus 2019 (COVID 19) for Child and Adolescent Mental Health," *Child and Adolescent Psychiatry and Mental Health* 14, no. 20 (2020).

42. Lauren Bauer, "The Covid 19 Crisis Has Already Left Too Many Children Hungry in America," Brookings Institution, May 12, 2020.

43. Sean F. Reardon, Joseph P. Robinson-Cimpian, and Erika S. Weathers, "Patterns and Trends in Racial/Ethnic and Socioeconomic Academic Achievement Gaps," in *Handbook of Research in Education Finance and Policy*, eds. Helen F. Ladd and Margaret E. Goertz (New York: Routledge, 2015), 491–509.

CHAPTER 4

1. Randy Capps et al., "Implications of Immigration Enforcement Activities for the Well-being of Children in Immigrant Families: A Review of the Literature," Urban Institute and Migration Policy Institute, September 2015, https://www.migration policy.org/research/implications-immigration-enforcement-activities-well-being -children-immigrant-families.

2. Lars Schwabe and Oliver T. Wolf, "Learning Under Stress Impairs Memory Formation," *Neurobiology of Learning and Memory* 93 (2010): 183–188; Steven Maier and Martin E. Seligman, "Learned Helplessness: Theory and Evidence," *Journal of Experimental Psychology* 105, no. 1 (1976): 3–46, https://doi.org/10.1037/0096-3445.105.1.3.

3. "Excessive Stress Disrupts the Architecture of the Developing Brain" (working paper no. 3, National Scientific Council on the Developing Child, Harvard University, Cambridge, MA, 2005), https://developingchild.harvard.edu/resources/wp3/.

4. "Persistent Fear and Anxiety Can Affect Young Children's Learning and Development," (working paper no. 9, National Scientific Council on the Developing Child, Harvard University, Cambridge, MA, 2010), http://www.developingchild.net.

5. Maier and Seligman, "Learned Helplessness."

6. Ross A. Thompson, "Stress and Child Development," *Future of Children* 24, no. 1 (2014): 41–59.

7. Ajay Chaudry et al., "Facing Our Future. Children in the Aftermath of Immigration Enforcement," The Urban Institute, February 2010, https://www.urban.org/sites /default/files/publication/28331/412020-Facing-Our-Future.PDF.

8. Catalina Amuedo-Dorantes and Mary J. Lopez, "The Hidden Educational Costs of Intensified Immigration Enforcement," *Southern Economic Journal* 84, no. 1 (2007): 120–154.

9. Nailing Xia and Sheila Nataraj Kirby, "Retaining Students in Grade: A literature review of the effects of retention on students' academic and non-academic outcomes," RAND Corporation Technical Report, 2009, http://www.rand.org/content/dam /rand/pubs/technical_reports/2009/RAND_TR678.pdf.

10. Martin Carnoy and Emma García, "Five Key Trends in U.S. Student Performance," Economic Policy Institute, January 12, 2017, https://www.epi.org/publication/five -key-trends-in-u-s-student-performance-progress-by-blacks-and-hispanics-the-takeoff -of-asians-the-stall-of-non-english-speakers-the-persistence-of-socioeconomic-gaps -and-the-damaging-effect/#epi-toc-14.

11. This is one of the major themes in Marcelo Suárez Orozco and Carola Suárez Orozco, *Transformations* (Palo Alto, CA: Stanford University Press, 1995), in which the authors interviewed many immigrant students about their school motivation.

12. Jie Zong et al., "A Profile of Current DACA Recipients by Education, Industry, and Occupation," Migration Policy Institute, November 2017, https://www.migration policy.org/research/profile-current-daca-recipients-education-industry-and-occupation.

13. Ruth Berkowitz et al., "A Research Synthesis of the Associations Between Socio-economic Background, Inequality, School Climate and Academic Achievement," *Review of Educational Research* 87 (2017): 425–469.

14. Berkowitz et al., "A Research Synthesis," 425–469.

15. Elizabeth Trovall, "A Year after Being Detained by ICE, a Houston High School Student Forges His Future," Houston Public Media, February 14, 2019, www.houston publicmedia.org/articles/news/politics/immigration/2019/02/12/321227/a-year-after -being-detained-by-ice-former-houston-high-school-student-forges-his-future/.

16. Claude Steele and Joshua Aronson, "Stereotype Threat and The Intellectual Test Performance of African Americans," *Journal of Personality and Social Psychology* 69, no. 5 (1995): 797–811; A. Joshua Aaronson, "The Threat of Stereotype," *Educational Leadership* 62, no. 3 (2004): 14–19.

17. Albert Bandura, *Self-Efficacy: The Exercise of Control* (New York: W. H. Freeman, 1997).

18. Herbert W. Marsh and Alison O'Mara, "Reciprocal Effects Between Academic Self-Concept, Self-Esteem, Achievement, and Attainment Over Seven Adolescent Years: Unidimensional and Multidimensional Perspectives of Self-Concept," *Personality & Social Psychology Bulletin* 34, no. 4 (2008): 542–552.

19. Patricia Gándara, Susan O'Hara, and Dianna Gutiérrez, "The Changing Shape of Aspirations," in *School Connections. US Mexican Youth, Peers, and School Achievement*, ed. Margaret Gibson et al. (New York: Teachers College Press, 2004), 39–62.

20. Carol Goodenow, "Classroom Belonging Among Early Adolescent Students: Relationships to Motivation and Achievement," *Journal of Early Adolescence* 13 (1993): 21–43; Carol Goodenow and Kathleen E. Grady, "The Relationship of School Belonging and Friends' Values to Academic Motivation Among Urban Adolescent Students," *Journal of Experimental Education* 62, no. 1 (1993): 60–71.

21. Gibson et al., *School Connections*; Guadalupe Espinoza and Jaana Juvonen, "Perceptions of the School Social Context Across the Transition to Middle School: Heightened Sensitivity Among Latino Students?," *Journal of Educational Psychology* 103 (2011): 749–758; Gladys E. Ibañez, Gabriel Kuperminc, and Greg Jurkovic, "Cultural Attributes and Adaptations Linked to Achievement Motivation Among Latino Adolescents," *Journal of Youth and Adolescence* 33 (2004): 559–568.

22. Gibson et al., *School Connections*.

23. Francis Huang and Dewey Cornell, "School Teasing and Bullying after the Presidential Election," *Educational Researcher* 48 (2019): 69–83.

24. John Rogers, "Teaching and Learning in the Age of Trump: Increasing Stress and Hostility in America's High Schools," UCLA Institute for Democracy, Education and Access, October 2017, https://idea.gseis.ucla.edu/publications/teaching-and-learning-in-age-of-trump.

25. William H. Jeynes, "A Meta-analysis—The Effects of Parental Involvement on Minority Children's Academic Achievement," *Education and Urban Society* 35 (2003): 202–218; William H. Jeynes, "A Meta-analysis—The Effects of Parental Involvement on Latino Student Outcomes," *Education and Urban Society* 49, no. 1 (2017): 4–28.

26. Annette Lareau and Erin McNamara Horvat, "Moments of Social Inclusion and Exclusion: Race, Class, and Cultural Capital in Family–School Relationships," *Sociology of Education* 72 (1999): 37–53.

27. Kristin Turney and Grace Kao, "Barriers to School Involvement: Are Immigrant Parents Disadvantaged?," *Journal of Educational Research* 102 (2009): 257–271; Carola Suárez-Orozco and Marcelo M. Suárez-Orozco, *Children of Immigration* (Cambridge, MA: Harvard University Press, 2001).

28. The Migration Policy Institute calculates that relatively few immigrants, estimated at 167,000, would actually be affected by the public charge rule because they aren't eligible for federal government services anyway; however, it could shape immigration for the future. See https://www.migrationpolicy.org/news/public-charge-denial-green-cards-benefits-use.

29. Anthony Bryk and Barbara Schneider, *Trust in Schools* (New York: Russell Sage, 2002).

30. Randy Capps et al. "Immigration Enforcement and the Mental Health of Latino High School Students," Migration Policy Institute, September 2020, https://www.migration policy.org/research/immigration-enforcement-mental-health-latino-students.

CHAPTER 5

1. This is the identical sample construction used in Thomas S. Dee and Mark Murphy, "Vanished Classmates: The Effects of Local Immigration Enforcement on School Enrollment," *American Educational Research Journal* 57, no. 2 (2020): 694–727.

2. Luis H. Zayas and Laurie Cook Heffron, "Disrupting Young Lives: How Detention and Deportation Affect US-Born Children of Immigrants," *American Psychological Association, Children Youth and Families News*, November 2016, 1–6.
3. Our Hispanic category includes all students who indicated Hispanic ethnicity. The non-Hispanic ethnicity category of students includes those students who did not mark Hispanic ethnicity and identified their race as American Indian/Alaska Native, Black, Native Hawaiian/Pacific Islander, or Black. We exclude students that indicated their race as Asian from this category. This exclusion is due to the preponderance of Asian immigrants among the population of undocumented residents. We also exclude the modestly sized "Two or More Races" category, which often includes individuals who report an Asian race as well as those who report "Some Other Race," a category that some Hispanic respondents choose.
4. J. David Brown et al., "Understanding the Quality of Alternative Citizenship Data Sources for the 2020 Census," US Census Bureau, Center for Economic Studies, Discussion Papers, 2018.
5. Dee and Murphy, "Vanished Classmates."
6. Dee and Murphy, "Vanished Classmates."
7. Richard O. Welsh, "School Hopscotch: A Comprehensive Review of K–12 Student Mobility in the United States," *Review of Educational Research* 87, no. 3 (2017): 475–511; Zeyu Xu, Jane Hannaway, and Stephanie D'Souza, "Student Transience in North Carolina: The Effect of School Mobility on Student Outcomes Using Longitudinal Data" (CALDER Working Paper No. 22, 2009); Russell W. Rumberger, "Student Mobility: Causes, Consequences, and Solutions," National Education Policy Center, Boulder, CO, 2015; Julie Berry Cullen et al., "What Can Be Done To Improve Struggling High Schools?," *Journal of Economic Perspectives* 27, no. 2 (2013): 133–152.
8. Jeffrey S. Passel and Paul Taylor, "Unauthorized Immigrants and Their U.S.-Born Children" (Washington, DC, 2010).
9. Ajay Chaudry et al., "Facing Our Future: Children in the Aftermath of Immigration Enforcement" (Washington, DC, The Urban Institute, 2010); Lisseth Rojas-Flores et al., "Trauma and Psychological Distress in Latino Citizen Children Following Parental Detention and Deportation," *Psychological Trauma: Theory, Research, Practice, and Policy* 9, no. 3 (2017): 352–361.
10. Jacob Rugh and Matthew Hall, "Deporting the American Dream: Immigration Enforcement and Latino Foreclosures," *Sociological Science* 3 (2016): 1053–1076; Scott D. Rhodes et al., "The Impact of Local Immigration Enforcement Policies on the Health of Immigrant Hispanics/Latinos in the United States," *American Journal of Public Health* 105, no. 2 (2015): 329–337; Stephanie Potochnick, Jen Hao Chen, and Krista Perreira, "Local-Level Immigration Enforcement and Food Insecurity Risk among Hispanic Immigrant Families with Children: National-Level Evidence," *Journal of Immigrant and Minority Health* 19, no. 5 (2017): 1042–1049; Aarti Shahani and Judith Greene, "Local Democracy on ICE: Why State and Local Governments Have No Business in Federal Immigration Law Enforcement," *A Justice Strategies Report*, 2009; Eric Garcetti, Mike Feuer, and Herb J. Wesson, "Letter to ICE from Los Angeles" (Los Angeles: City of Los Angeles, 2017); Genti Kostandini, Elton Mykerezi,

and Cesar Escalante, "The Impact of Immigration Enforcement on the U.S. Farming Sector," *American Journal of Agricultural Economics* 96, no. 1 (2014): 172–192; Huyen Pham and Pham Hoang Van, "The Economic Impact of Local Immigration Regulation: An Empirical Analysis," *Cardozo Law Review* 32, no. 2 (2010): 485–518; Andrew Forrester and Alex Nowrasteh, "Do Immigration Enforcement Programs Reduce Crime? Evidence from the 287(g) Program in North Carolina" (CATO working paper, 2018).

11. Specifically, there were two ways that a school could classify as a Title I–eligible school. First, the school was flagged by the National Center for Education Statistics (NCES) as simply being a "Title I–Eligible School." This means the school received some formula funding through Title I because of the enrollment of low-income students. Second, the school was flagged by NCES as having a "Schoolwide Title I" program. This meant that more than 40% of the student body of the school qualified as low-income students.

12. Importantly, our sample includes Los Angeles County, which influences our summary statistics.

13. US Citizen and Immigration Services, "E-Verify Participating Employers," 2018.

14. Donald Trump, "Executive Order 13767 of January 25, 2017: Border Security and Immigration Enforcement Improvements," 82 Federal Register § (2017).

15. Data on immigration detainers were collected from the US Department of Homeland Security by the Transactional Records Access Clearinghouse (TRAC) at Syracuse Univesrity. TRAC generously shared these data with us to conduct these analyses.

16. For methodological details, please see the "Method" section of Dee and Murphy, "Vanished Classmates." Specifically, we rely on equations (1), (2), and (3) as our main specifications for this chapter.

17. The increase observed the year before treatment may stem from the way we define treatment (i.e., agreements established before October 1 are flagged as part of a particular school year; those established after October 1 are flagged as part of the subsequent school year).

18. Jeffrey S. Passel and D'Vera Cohn, "A Portrait of Unauthorized Immigrants in the United States," *Pew Research Center Report* (Washington, DC, 2009).

19. Dee and Murphy, "Vanished Classmates."

20. Tara Watson, "Enforcement and Immigrant Location Choice" (NBER Working Paper Series, Cambridge, MA, 2013; Kostandini, Mykerezi, and Escalante, "The Impact of Immigration Enforcement on the U.S. Farming Sector"; Kevin S. O'Neil, "Immigration Enforcement by Local Police under 287(g) and Growth of Unauthorized Immigrant and Other Populations" (SSRN Working Paper, 2013); E. A. Parrado, "Immigration Enforcement Policies, the Economic Recession, and the Size of Local Mexican Immigrant Populations," *ANNALS of the American Academy of Political and Social Science* 641, no. 1 (2012): 16–37.

21. Sean F. Reardon et al., "Is Separate Still Unequal? New Evidence on School Segregation and Racial Academic Achievement Gaps" (CEPA working paper, Stanford, CA, 2019).

22. Dee and Murphy, "Vanished Classmates."

23. Passel and Cohn, "A Portrait of Unauthorized Immigrants in the United States."

24. Welsh, "School Hopscotch: A Comprehensive Review of K–12 Student Mobility in the United States"; Xu, Hannaway, and D'Souza, "Student Transience in North Carolina: The Effect of School Mobility on Student Outcomes Using Longitudinal Data"; Rumberger, "Student Mobility: Causes, Consequences, and Solutions"; Alexandra Beatty, *Student Mobility: Exploring the Impacts of Frequent Moves on Achievement: Summary of a Workshop* (Washington, DC: The National Academies Press, 2010).

25. Chaudry et al., "Facing Our Future: Children in the Aftermath of Immigration Enforcement"; Rojas-Flores et al., "Trauma and Psychological Distress in Latino Citizen Children Following Parental Detention and Deportation."

26. Cullen et al., "What Can Be Done To Improve Struggling High Schools?"

27. Rugh and Hall, "Deporting the American Dream: Immigration Enforcement and Latino Foreclosures"; Potochnick, Chen, and Perreira, "Local-Level Immigration Enforcement and Food Insecurity Risk among Hispanic Immigrant Families with Children: National-Level Evidence"; Rhodes et al., "The Impact of Local Immigration Enforcement Policies on the Health of Immigrant Hispanics/Latinos in the United States"; Pham and Van, "The Economic Impact of Local Immigration Regulation: An Empirical Analysis"; Kostandini, Mykerezi, and Escalante, "The Impact of Immigration Enforcement on the U.S. Farming Sector."

28. Forrester and Nowrasteh, "Do Immigration Enforcement Programs Reduce Crime? Evidence from the 287(g) Program in North Carolina."

29. Shahani and Greene, "Local Democracy on ICE: Why State and Local Governments Have No Business in Federal Immigration Law Enforcement"; Garcetti, Feuer, and Wesson, "Letter to ICE from Los Angeles."

30. Patricia G. Devine et al., "Long-Term Reduction in Implicit Race Bias: A Prejudice Habit-Breaking Intervention," *Journal of Experimental Social Psychology* 48, no. 6 (2012): 1267–1278; Thomas F. Pettigrew et al., "Recent Advances in Intergroup Contact Theory," *International Journal of Intercultural Relations* 35, no. 3 (2011): 271–280; Thomas F. Pettigrew and Linda R. Tropp, "A Meta-Analytic Test of Intergroup Contact Theory," *Journal of Personality and Social Psychology* 90, no. 5 (2006): 751–783.

31. Angela Garcia, "Treating Toxic Stress in Immigrant Children," *National Association of School Psychologists* 46, no. 7 (2016): 30–32; US Department of Education, "What Works Clearinghouse: Children Classified as Having an Emotional Disturbance: First Step to Success," What Works Clearinghouse, 2012; S. Baker et al., "Teaching Academic Content and Literacy to English Language Learners in Elementary and Middle School" (Washington, DC, 2014).

32. Zayas and Cook Heffron, "Disrupting Young Lives: How Detention and Deportation Affect US-Born Children of Immigrants."

33. Vanessa Ríos-Salas and Andrea Larson, "Perceived Discrimination, Socioeconomic Status, and Mental Health among Latino Adolescents in US Immigrant Families," *Children and Youth Services Review* (Madison, WI: Elsevier Science, 2015).

CHAPTER 6

1. Caitlin Dickerson and Kirk Semple, "U.S. Deported Thousands Amid Covid-19 Outbreak. Some Proved to Be Sick," *New York Times*, April 18, 2020, https://www.nytimes.com/2020/04/18/us/deportations-coronavirus-guatemala.html.

2. John Rogers et al., *Teaching and Learning in the Age of Trump: Increasing Stress and Hostility in America's High Schools* (Los Angeles: UCLA Institute for Democracy, Education and Access, 2017), https://idea.gseis.ucla.edu/publications/teaching-and-learning-in-age-of-trump.

3. We use the Migration Policy Institute's definition of children of immigrants (or children in immigrant families) to refer to immigrant students as "children under 18 with at least one immigrant parent"; we also include students who are "residing in the United States who were not U.S. citizens at birth."

4. Jongyeon Ee and Patricia Gándara, "The Impact of Immigration Enforcement on the Nation's Schools," *American Educational Research Journal* 57, no. 2 (April 2020): 840–871, doi:10.3102/0002831219862998.

5. National Child Traumatic Stress Network, Secondary Traumatic Stress Committee, "Secondary Traumatic Stress: A Fact Sheet for Child-Serving Professionals" (Los Angeles, and Durham, NC: National Center for Child Traumatic Stress, 2011); Sarah Peterson, "Secondary Traumatic Stress," Text, The National Child Traumatic Stress Network, January 30, 2018, https://www.nctsn.org/trauma-informed-care/secondary-traumatic-stress.

6. Jason M. Newell and Gordon A. MacNeil, "Professional Burnout, Vicarious Trauma, Secondary Traumatic Stress, and Compassion Fatigue," *Best Practices in Mental Health* 6 (2010): 58.

7. Joan C. Tronto, *Moral Boundaries: A Political Argument for an Ethic of Care* (New York: Routledge, 1993); Joan C. Tronto, "Care as a Political Concept," in *Revisioning the Political* (New York: Routledge, 2018), 139–156.

8. Herbert J. Freudenberger, "Burnout: Past, Present, and Future Concerns," *Loss, Grief & Care* 3, no. 1–2 (1989): 1–10.

9. Vivienne Collinson and Tanya Fedoruk Cook, "'I Don't Have Enough Time'—Teachers' Interpretations of Time as a Key to Learning and School Change," *Journal of Educational Administration* 39, no. 3 (2001): 266–281, doi: 10.1108/09578230110392884.

10. Ee and Gándara. "The Impact of Immigration."

11. Gary Orfield and Chungmei Lee, *Why Segregation Matters: Poverty and Educational Inequality* (Cambridge, MA: Civil Rights Project at Harvard University, 2005); Anthony Bryk and Barbara Schneider, "Trust in Schools: A Core Resource for Improvement," Rose Series in Sociology, American Sociological Association (Russell Sage Foundation, 2002); Angela Valenzuela and Brenda Rubio, "Subtractive Schooling," *The TESOL Encyclopedia of English Language Teaching*, 2018, 1–7, doi: 10.1002/9781118784235.eelt0139.

12. Bryk and Schneider, *Trust in Schools*; Nermeen E. El Nokali, Heather J. Bachman, and Elizabeth Votruba-Drzal, "Parent Involvement and Children's Academic and Social Development in Elementary School," *Child Development* 81, no. 3 (2010): 988–1005, doi: 10.1111/j.1467-8624.2010.01447.x.

13. Newell and MacNeil, "Professional Burnout, Vicarious Trauma, Secondary Traumatic Stress, and Compassion Fatigue."

14. Jihyun Kim, Peter Youngs, and Kenneth Frank, "Burnout Contagion: Is It Due to Early Career Teachers' Social Networks or Organizational Exposure?," *Teaching and Teacher Education* 66 (2017): 250–260, doi: 10.1016/j.tate.2017.04.017.

CHAPTER 7

1. Given that different-sized districts would presumably have different administrative structures and different levels of resources, we also included various sizes of districts, including five large, five medium, and seven small districts based on the total enrollment.

2. Because notaries or *notarios públicos* have a more official role in Mexico and other Latin American countries, immigrants are often duped into believing that the notary can conduct immigration business for them, including acquiring citizenship on their behalf.

3. Communities in Schools, Communitiesinschools.org.

4. A Broader, Bolder Approach to Education, Boldapproach.org.

5. Ernesto Castañeda et al., "The Movement for Immigrant Rights," in *Social Movements 1768–2018*, eds. Charles Tilly, Ernesto Castañeda, and Lesley Wood (New York: Routledge, 2020), 177–193.

CHAPTER 8

1. Hiroshi Motomura, "Arguing About Sanctuary," *UC Davis Law Review* 52 (2018): 435.

2. Marco A. Murillo, "UndocuCollege Access: Addressing Documentation Issues in the College Choice Process," in *Educational Leadership of Immigrants: Case Studies in Times of Change*, eds. Emily R. Crawford and Lisa M. Dorner (New York: Routledge, 2019), 79; Michael Olivas. *Perchance to DREAM: A Legal and Political History of the DREAM Act and DACA.* (New York: NYU Press, 2020).

3. United Nations High Commissioner for Refugees, *Children On the Run: Unaccompanied Children Leaving Central America and Mexico and the Need for International Protection* (Geneva: The UN Refuge Agency, 2014), https://www.unhcr.org/56fc266f4.html.

4. Mark Warren, "Communities and Schools: A New View of Urban Education Reform," *Harvard Educational Review* 75 (2005): 133.

5. Reuben Jacobson et al., "It Takes A Community," *Phi Delta Kappan* 99 (2018): 8.

6. Marcelo Suárez-Orozco and Carola Suárez-Orozco, "Children of Immigration: The Story of Children of Immigration Is Deeply Intertwined with the Future of Our Nation," *Phi Delta Kappan* 97 (2015): 8.

7. Ramon Antonio Martinez and Karen Hunter Quartz, "Zoned for Change: A Historical Case Study of the Belmont Zone of Choice," *Teachers College Record* 114 (2012): n10.

8. Data based on the American Community Survey (ACS) about children by nativity of parents by age group. These are five-year estimates (2014–2018) shown by tract, county, and state boundaries. Source accessed from UCLA Data for Democracy Brief: Immigration In LA. https://centerx.gseis.ucla.edu/data-for-democracy/briefs/immigration-in-la/.

9. Los Angeles Unified School District, "LA Unified Campuses as Safe Zones and Resource Centers for Students and Families Threatened by Immigration Enforcement" (Los Angeles: LAUSD, 2016), http://laschoolboard.org/.

10. Alan Berube, "Sanctuary Cities and Trump's Executive Order," Brookings, February 24, 2017, https://www.brookings.edu/blog/unpacked/2017/02/24/sanctuary-cities-and-trumps-executive-order/.

11. Los Angeles Unified School District, "Reaffirmation of LA Unified Campuses as Safe Zones and Resource Centers for Students and Families Threatened by Immigration Enforcement," (Los Angeles: LAUSD, 2017), http://laschoolboard.org/.

12. Los Angeles Unified School District, *Reaffirmation*, 3.

13. Los Angeles Unified School District, *Reaffirmation*.

14. Karen Hunter Quartz et al., "Framing, Supporting, and Tracking College-For-All Reform: A Local Case of Public Scholarship," *High School Journal* 102, no. 2) (2019): 159–182.

15. Ann M. Ishimaru and Sola Takahashi, "Disrupting Racialized Institutional Scripts: Toward Parent–Teacher Transformative Agency for Educational Justice," *Peabody Journal of Education* 92 (2017): 343; Karen L. Mapp and Paul J. Kuttner, "Partners in Education: A Dual Capacity-Building Framework for Family-School Partnerships," Southwest Educational Development Laboratory, 2014.

16. Kevin Kane, Karen Hunter Quartz, and Lindsey Kunisaki, "Multigenerational Art Making at a Community School: A Case Study of Transformative Parent Engagement," Manuscript submitted for publication.

17. Kane et al., "Multigenerational Art."

18. Cecilia Menjivar and Nina Rabin, "Youth on Their Own," in *Illegal Encounters: The Effect of Detention and Deportation on Young People*, eds. Deborah A. Boehm and Susan J. Terrio (New York: NYU Press, 2019), 89.

19. Bruce Katz and Jeremy Nowak, *The New Localism: How Cities Can Thrive in the Age of Populism* (Washington, DC: Brookings Institution Press, 2017).

20. Katz and Nowak, *The New Localism*.

21. Tanya Golash-Boza and Zulema Valdez, "Nested Contexts of Reception: Undocumented Students at the University of California, Central," *Sociological Perspectives* 61 (2018): 535.

22. Pratheepan Gulasekaram, Rick Su, and Rose Cuison Villazor, "Anti-Sanctuary and Immigration Localism," *Columbia Law Review* 119 (2019): 837.

23. Carola Suárez-Orozco et al., "Growing Up in the Shadows: The Developmental Implications of Unauthorized Status," *Harvard Educational Review* 81 (2011): 438.

24. Leigh Patel, "Immigrant Populations and Sanctuary Schools," *Journal of Literacy Research* 50 (2018): 524.

CHAPTER 9

1. Randy Capps et al., "Immigration Enforcement and the Mental Health of Latino High School Students" (Washington, DC: Migration Policy Institute, September 2020).

2. Parent Institute for Quality Education, Piqe.org.

3. Section 504 of the Rehabilitation Act of 1973 provides resources for students with more mild or ephemeral handicaps that do not require an Individualized Educational Plan (IEP). These funds could be used for students who have been victims of various kinds of trauma.

4. Immschools.org is a nonprofit created by formerly undocumented students that works with districts to provide information and support for teachers of immigrant and undocumented students.

5. Jens Manuel Krogstad, "Americans Broadly Support Legal Status for Immigrants Brought to the U.S. Illegally as Children," Pew Research Center, June 17, 2020, https://www.pewresearch.org/fact-tank/2020/06/17/americans-broadly-support-legal-status-for-immigrants-brought-to-the-u-s-illegally-as-children/.

ABOUT THE EDITORS

PATRICIA GÁNDARA is research professor and codirector of the Civil Rights Project at UCLA. She is also director of education for the University of California–Mexico Initiative. Gándara is a 2019 recipient of the Alfonso Garcia Robles medal, conferred by the National Autonomous University of Mexico (UNAM) for work on behalf of Mexican immigrants in the United States. She is also an elected fellow of the American Educational Research Association (AERA) and of the National Academy of Education. In 2011, she was appointed to President Obama's Commission on Educational Excellence for Hispanics and, in 2015, received the Distinguished Career Award from the Scholars of Color Committee of the American Educational Research Association. In 2016, she gave the first AERA Centennial lecture at the Brooklyn Museum entitled, "Educating Immigrant students and English learners in an anti-immigrant era." She has also been a fellow of the Rockefeller Foundation Bellagio Center in Italy, the French-American Association at Sciences Po Graduate Institute, Paris, and an ETS fellow at Princeton, New Jersey. She has written or edited eight books and published over 150 articles, chapters, and major policy reports. She has written chapters in several Harvard Education Press edited books, including "On Nobody's Agenda" (Sadowski, 2004); "English Learners, Immigrant Students, and the Challenge of Time" (Saunders et al., 2017); "Deeper Learning for English Language Learners" (Heller et al., 2017).

Her most recent books include *The Students We Share: Preparing US and Mexican Teachers for Our Transnational Future*, with Bryant Jensen (SUNY, 2021); *The Bilingual Advantage: Language, Literacy, and the U.S. Labor Market*, with Rebecca Callahan (Multilingual Matters, 2014); *Forbidden*

Language, with Megan Hopkins (Teachers College Press, 2010); and *The Latino Education Crisis*, with Frances Contreras (Harvard University Press, 2009). Most recent published articles include "The Economic Value of Bilingualism in the United States (*Bilingual Research Journal*, 2018); "The Students We Share: Falling through the Cracks on Both Sides of the US-Mexican Border" (*Ethnic and Racial Studies*, 2019); "The Impact of Immigration Enforcement on the Nation's Schools," with J. Ee (*American Educational Research Journal*, 2019); "What Shall Be the Future for the Children of Migration?," in *Equitable Globalization*, ed. E. Tellez and R. Hinojosa, University of California Press, in press); and "Betraying Our Immigrant Students" (*Kappan*, September 2018).

JONGYEON EE is an assistant professor at the School of Education, Loyola Marymount University (LMU). She earned her doctorate from the UCLA Graduate School of Education and was a postdoctoral research associate at the UCLA Civil Rights Project. She has authored several research reports and book chapters on school segregation, racial inequality, and school discipline in K–12 schools, including "Harming Our Common Future: America's Segregated Schools 65 Years after Brown," "Segregating California's Future: Inequality and Its Alternative 60 Years after *Brown v. Board of Education*," and "Our Segregated Capital: An Increasingly Diverse City with Racially Polarized Schools." Her recent publications have also focused on language-minority students and immigrant students and have appeared in *American Educational Research Journal*, *Bilingual Research Journal*, and *International Journal of Bilingualism and Bilingual Education*, including "The Impact of Immigration Enforcement on the Nation's Schools," "10 Employer Preferences: Do Bilingual Applicants and Employees Experience an Advantage?," "Are Parents Satisfied with Integrated Classrooms?: Exploring Integration in Dual Language Programs," and "Bamboo Bridges or Barriers? Exploring Advantages of Bilingualism among Asians in the US Labor Market Through the Lens of Superdiversity." She was awarded the Outstanding Dissertation Award from the National Association for Bilingual Education and the Ascending Scholar Award form LMU.

ABOUT THE CONTRIBUTORS

THOMAS S. DEE, PhD, is the Barnett Family Professor at Stanford University's Graduate School of Education, a research associate at the National Bureau of Economic Research, and a senior fellow at the Stanford Institute for Economic Policy Research. He also is the faculty director of the John W. Gardner Center for Youth and Their Communities. His research focuses largely on the use of quantitative methods to inform contemporary issues of policy and practice. Recent examples include studies of curricular innovations in Bay Area school districts, studies of accountability policies, and ongoing research on how interior immigration enforcement has influenced students and schools.

RACHEL FREEMAN, MA, is a PhD candidate in the Graduate School of Education and Information Studies at the University of California, Los Angeles, where she is also a research associate for the Institute for Immigration, Globalization, and Education. Rachel's research interests include access and equity in higher education for immigrant and undocumented students. Rachel has worked extensively with immigrant advocacy organizations including *My Undocumented Life Blog* and UndocuScholars, and has worked in the higher-education sector for Bunker Hill Community College, MassBay Community College, Harvard's Graduate School of Education, Achieving the Dream, and Jobs for the Future. She received her master's in higher education from Harvard's Graduate School of Education and her bachelor's in philosophy from The University of Chicago.

LEYDA W. GARCIA, EdD, is the principal of the UCLA Community School and part of the Principal Leadership Institute faculty at UCLA School of Education and Information Studies. She has been an educator for over twenty years. Her ideal classroom represents a space full of possibilities to transgress and to make education *the practice of freedom* (hooks, 1994). Dr. Garcia is an ardent advocate for subaltern voices in the field, from immigrant students to students with disabilities. Her social justice orientation guides her shared-leadership approach to create vibrant school communities where all voices are heard and elevated. She holds a BA in psychology, an MA in education from Stanford University, an MEd in education from UCLA, and an EdD from Loyola Marymount University. As a researcher and scholar Dr. Garcia focuses on the experiences of immigrant-origin youth, YPAR methodologies, and school leadership.

KAREN HUNTER QUARTZ, PhD, is director of the UCLA Center for Community Schooling and is a faculty member in the UCLA School of Education & Information Studies. Her research, teaching, and service support community school development, teacher autonomy and retention, and educational reform. Professor Quartz led the design team in 2007 to create the UCLA Community School and served in 2017 on the design team for a second site, the Mann UCLA Community School. She currently oversees a portfolio of research-practice partnerships at both schools designed to advance democracy, inquiry, and change. She is recipient of the 2001 Outstanding Book Award from the American Educational Research Association, the 2004 Outstanding Writing Award from the American Association of Colleges of Teacher Education, and the 2017 National Teacher-Powered Schools Initiative's Advancement in Research Award. She holds a BA from Huron College, an MA in philosophy from the University of Western Ontario, and a PhD in education from the University of California, Los Angeles.

PATRICIA MARTÍN, MA, is a fourth-year doctoral student in the Graduate School of Education & Information Studies (GSE&IS) at UCLA where she is currently a research assistant for the Enrollment Management, Recruiting, and Access research project. Patricia's research interests focus on the intersection of college access and organizational behavior. She is interested in using computational social science methods to investigate the digital marketing strategies of postsecondary institutions and their effects on college access for underserved students. She received her master's of arts in education from UCLA and her bachelor's in sociology from UC Santa Barbara.

MARCO A. MURILLO, PhD, is an assistant professor of Education in the School of Education and Counseling Psychology at Santa Clara University. His research examines the ways the K–16 school system meets and/or fails to meet the academic and social needs of traditionally underserved students by investigating the interplay between institutional structures, agency, race, legal status, and culture in shaping students' secondary and postsecondary educational outcomes. He holds a BA in political science and history from the University of California San Diego and a PhD in Education (urban schooling) from the University of California, Los Angeles.

MARK MURPHY, PhD, is an assistant professor at the University of Hawai'i at Mānoa's College of Education. His research focuses on educational equity, immigration policy, multilingual students, and school finance, with an emphasis on the implications of federal policies on educational outcomes. Prior to joining the University of Hawai'i at Mānoa, he was an Institute of Education Sciences Fellow at Stanford University's Graduate School of Education.

NINA RABIN, JD, is director of the Immigrant Family Legal Clinic at UCLA School of Law. In the legal clinic, Professor Rabin works in partnership with community organizations and local institutions to best serve the multifaceted needs of mixed-status families. At the same time, she has undertaken policy research and advocacy to study and document the impact of immigration enforcement on young people and families. She has authored articles and reports on the consequences of immigration enforcement for children in immigrant families, working conditions of immigrant women workers, immigrants' parental rights, and the treatment of women fleeing gender-based violence in immigration detention. She has spoken extensively on immigration policy issues in a variety of venues, including academic conferences, community forums, and a congressional briefing. She has also participated in trainings on immigration for attorneys and community leaders.

SHENA SANCHEZ, PhD, is an assistant professor of qualitative inquiry at the University of Alabama. She received her PhD in Urban Schooling from the University of California, Los Angeles, an MEd in international education policy and management from Vanderbilt University, and a BA in English with a minor in Spanish from Roanoke College.

INDEX

mental health issues, 72. *See also* psycho-
social stress of students
Mexican consulates, 146
Meyer v. Nebraska (1923), 24
migration, increase in, 7–8
moving, 58, 95–96, 111
Multigenerational Afterschool Arts
(MASA) Program, 164–168

national identity, immigration seen as
threat to, 14–15
national origin quotas, 17, 19
national security, immigration seen as
threat to, 16, 21–23
newcomers, 155, 162
No Child Left Behind Act, 61
nutrition, 72, 88–89

Obama administration
deportation during, 3
"felons not families" policy, 3, 22–23,
27, 100
ICE-police partnerships, 94, 98
immigration reform, 3–4
OECD (Organization for Economic Cooperation and Development), 64
Operation Wetback, 18
opportunity gaps, 59, 69, 73, 79–80
Organization for Economic Cooperation and Development (OECD),
64
outreach to community. *See* community
outreach

pandemic of 2020, 32, 71–73, 172–173
parent engagement
educator comments about, 88–91
immigrant students, issues with, 59
information about how schools work,
177
survey results about, 38, 41, 44–45
Title I status and, 67, 70–71
transformative family engagement,
164–166
trust and, 124–125, 142

Parent Institute for Quality Education
(PIQE), 177
partnerships between ICE and local law
enforcement. *See* ICE-police
partnerships
Patel, Leigh, 170
philanthropy, 178
Plessy v. Ferguson (1896), 17
Plyler v. Doe (1982), 26–27
political differences, 45–47, 149, 169
population growth, 16
poverty. *See also* Title I schools
demographics, 58
English language learners and, 64–66
ICE-police partnerships and, 94–95, 107
support services for, 139–141,
143–145, 176–177
War on Poverty, 60, 63
principals, role, 135–136
Priority Enforcement Program, 100
professional development, 128, 141–142,
178–179
property taxes for school funding, 63
psychologists, 51
psychosocial stress of educators, 117–120,
126–127, 174
psychosocial stress of students
educator comments about, 76–78
ICE-police partnerships and, 111
impact on educators of, 118
prevalence of, 173–174
schools as critical for, 172–173
survey results about, 37–38, 43–44,
52–53
Title I status and, 67–68

raids
educator philosophy clarified by,
138–139
history of, 18, 20
negative impacts on students of, 5,
128–129
response plans, 148
school climate and, 69
self-deportation due to, 19